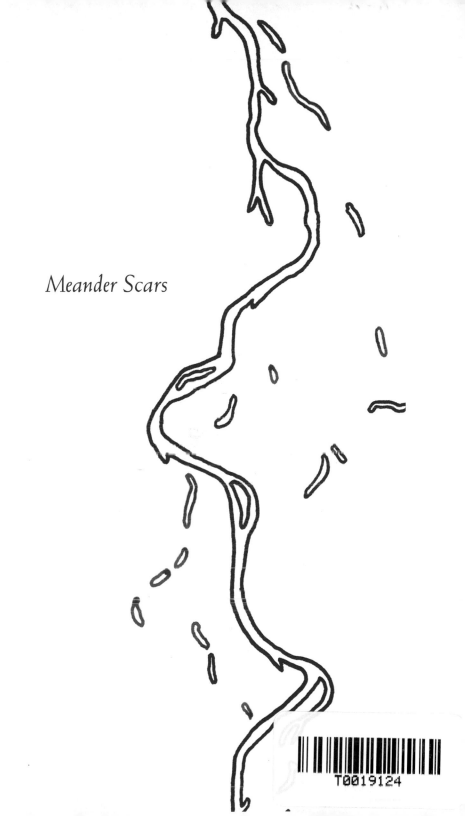

Meander Scars

Meander Scars

Reflections on Healing the Willamette River

❖❖❖

Abby P. Metzger

Oregon State University Press ❖❖❖ Corvallis

The paper in this book meets the guidelines for permanence and durability of the Committee on Production Guidelines for Book Longevity of the Council on Library Resources and the minimum requirements of the American National Standard for Permanence of Paper for Printed Library Materials Z39.48-1984.

Library of Congress Cataloging-in-Publication Data
Metzger, Abby P.
  Meander scars : reflections on healing the Willamette / Abby P. Metzger.
    pages cm
  Includes bibliographical references.
  ISBN 978-0-87071-726-0 (alkaline paper) -- ISBN 978-0-87071-727-7 (ebook)
  1. Restoration ecology--Oregon--Willamette River. 2. Stream ecology--Oregon--Willamette River. 3. Stream conservation--Oregon--Willamette River. 4. Environmental degradation--Oregon--Willamette River. 5. Willamette River (Or.)--History. 6. Metzger, Abby P.--Travel--Oregon--Willamette River. 7. Willamette River (Or.)--Description and travel. 8. Willamette River (Or.)--Environmental conditions. I. Title.
  QH105.O7M38 2013
  577.6'4097953--dc23
                          2013013097

Oregon State University Press
121 The Valley Library
Corvallis OR 97331-4501
541-737-3166 • fax 541-737-3170
www.osupress.oregonstate.edu

For my grandfather, J. K. Ward

❖❖❖

The Willamette River, Oregon

Pioneering research by Sedell and Froggatt illustrated the significant channel loss during and after European settlement between the McKenzie River confluence and Harrisburg.

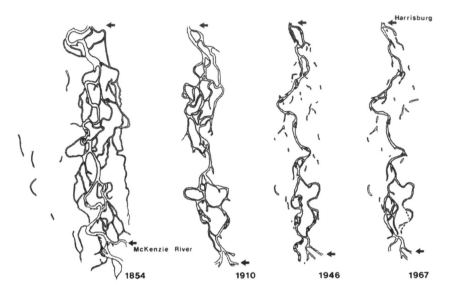

Reprinted with permission (original map found in Sedell, J. R. & Froggatt, J. L. [1984]. Importance of streamside forests to large rivers: The isolation of the Willamette River, Oregon, U.S.A., from its floodplain by snagging and streamside forest removal. *Verb. Internat. Verin. Limnol,* 22, 1828-1834.)

The Willamette River as of 2011

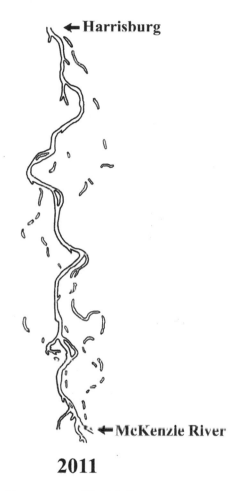

←Harrisburg

←McKenzie River

2011

Map courtesy of Patricia Benner.

Contents

.

Introduction

❖❖❖

I live by a river that flows through a broad valley between two mountain ranges, a river called the Willamette. Many times I've sat at its banks skipping stones, or strolled down a nearby footpath flanked by maple and ash trees. I've walked the riverside path with my family since I was a little girl.

One of my earliest memories is of my father crossing an errant channel of the Willamette clutching two small girls, my sister in one arm and me in the other. It must have been winter. He and my mother had traversed a rivulet and headed home a different way before realizing they would have to ford a much deeper channel. Rather than turning back, my father told us to stay put as he draped my mother across his arms and waded the river. Then he came for us. With my father holding me tight, I felt the strange and dueling tug of terror and calm, the natural lure of water and simultaneous fear-spun repulsion of it. To a small child, the water was swift and deep, but as long as I felt the strong grip of my father's hands and kept hold of my mother's eyes looking from the opposite shore, I would be fine, I told myself.

"Weren't you afraid?" I asked my father, almost twenty-five years after the incident.

"Good god, I was in my thirties then," he said. "I could swim like a sonofabitch."

And he could.

Even now, sometimes, the fear and calm, the pull of alarm and wonder come back to me when I watch the Willamette slosh against sandy banks with brown water. Maybe those opposing emotions are what keep me coming back to this river, again and again, sitting and watching even as my rear gets soaked from damp gravel. Maybe the alluring complexity of that early experience is partly why I stay in the town where I was born.

❖ ❖ ❖

Today I sit on a gravel bar and watch herons fly through cottonwoods and in between their knotted nests. The day is hazy and washed out, but the river surges. Its surface holds a light stronger than the sky.

I am alone, but not lonely enough to believe I am the only person to have sat on this shore. I can imagine a Kalapuya boy fishing along this edge of rock and water. Near here, European settlers pressed their boots into the nearby soil—men like Joseph C. Avery and William F. Dixon. When they came, these settlers left more than boot prints. They left legacy and ecological disgrace, a tamed river, productive cities, livelihood, loss, and safety. And years later, we're still following in their boot prints, hoping for a modicum of happiness and comfort.

Yet that is not all I imagine while watching the river. I can picture nineteenth-century Oregon poet laureate Samuel Simpson sitting in this spot and composing his "Beautiful Willamette," a pastoral poem about a river that threads across a valley floor before spilling into the Columbia and surging to the sea. Like me, Simpson must have felt his heart sing every time he watched the mighty Willamette and its marble surface. Today I can see the river just as Simpson wrote about it, "Waltzing, flashing / Tinkling, splashing ... / Always hurried / To be buried / In the bitter, moon-mad sea." Somehow, the river carries light even when the world is grey.

What Simpson didn't write about was how we have wronged this river, those lapping shadows of progress. He didn't write about the big eighteen-wheeler lugging gravel behind the heron rookery. He didn't live long enough to write about the plume of steam and whatever else coming from the Evanite Fiber Corporation beside the river. When he sat here—pretending for a moment that he did—Simpson likely didn't see a swath of sky filtering through the thin line of trees in front of me right now. Surely, the thick woods of his day let in only glints of daylight. Simpson didn't live long enough to see city grids bury the river's channels or the construction of Interstate 5. He never saw the twenty-foot rock wall that lines the Corvallis riverfront and keeps the Willamette from "waltzing." What kind of poem would Simpson write today? Would it be reverent, or full of guilt and sorrow?

Simpson got many things right in his poem, but one thing he got wrong was his assumption that this river would never be wounded. "Time that scars us, / Maims and mars us, / Leaves no track or trace on thee!" he wrote. He's right about time scarring us, leaving us at the mercy of passing moments and an inevitable end. But time has also scarred the river.

The Willamette River's scars can be seen across the valley floor. Rivers naturally erode on their outside bends, creating a rounded curve called a meander. Sometimes the river meander breaks away, abandoning the main channel and becoming a horseshoe-shaped lake, called an oxbow. When the stranded water dries, the oxbow becomes a meander scar, or the remnants of a wandering water channel.

The term "meander scar" is puzzling because a scar is a sign of wound repair. It's what time and the healing power of the earth have made of a harm, which suggests humans see rivers as inflictors of wounds that need healing. But I think this is all wrong. The real wounds—the real acts of harm in need of reconciliation—are the ones we've inflicted on this river, like draining, filling, and building over channels. Through the years, some channels vanished under concrete. Others became meander scars, those reminders of *our* hurt, those faint depressions in the land that still bear a shadowy resemblance to a river.

I've researched how the Willamette's channels either disappeared or became meander scars, wondering what kind of redemptive act could undo this harm. And in my research, I realized how much I still had to learn about the history underneath my feet, despite years of playing by the water and skimming stones across its dappled surface, despite the river forming the bedrock of my memories. Sometimes my love of this place, though genuine and deep rooted, felt misunderstood, because I was caring for a thing I knew little about. The river's pent-up rhythms of its former wildness, or the way it used to flood and create channels from year to year, were big mysteries. I did not live in acceptance of its cycles or understand the elusive beauty of a river both stunning and flawed. The more I learned, the more I felt something inside me was also severed and scarred, in need of time and contemplation to heal.

To make up for ecological loss, environmental groups are now proposing ways to reconnect former channels; in the same way I am searching for ways to reconnect to the river of my birthplace. I want to expose my life, bare root, to the messages of the Willamette and let river water spill into untraveled places. I have an urge to learn the meaning within an eddy's quiet swirl, or understand the power of a fish cutting upstream. There must be some lesson about awe hidden in the mist lifting from a stream, or that line of light carried downriver. What I hope to find is the restorative power of the river's washing, to come to a place of recovery, both for the Willamette and my relationship to it. By chance I might cross an errant channel and come to places new and unexpected, places of healing carried by uncut wonder and fear of a thing bigger than a single human existence.

In this book, I explore a simple question with no single answer: how can we heal a river and our relationship to it? In answering that question, I take an apprentice's journey through soggy backchannels, researching long-standing histories, ambling in creeks, overturning rocks, and reflecting on age-old mysteries about nature and our place in the world. What follows is the result of that reckless curiosity, the stories and experiences of a learner that I hope encourage the fellow uninitiated to get their feet wet.

If this book were a river, it would move from the headwaters of loss to the ocean-bound surge of reconciliation. I begin with the history of the Willamette, when it was wild and free, and move into all the ways we scarred it. The story then riffles and spills into a series of quiet pools where I reflect on what values might inform our restoration efforts: values such as complexity; values such as memories and stories that hold the history of a landscape before it was degraded; and finally, values such as grief and danger, which have brought me closer to this river in unexpected ways. In the final reach of the book, I delve into the ecological and philosophical dimensions of restoration. Using my own journey to more fully understand and care for the Willamette, I explore not just whether the physical process of restoration can assure future ecological certainty, but whether working to repair the earth truly compensates for our misdeeds, and whether restoration is a reflexive act where both participant and landscape are made anew.

❖❖❖

Not long after I started this project, I dreamed I walked barefoot to the Willamette's shore. Tall willows crosshatched a full moon that spilled wet light into shadows. I climbed a tree and sat on top of it, like John Muir did to watch a windstorm. From above, flecks of starlight sprinkled the land. From below, the water washed colorful stones that hissed at the current's touch, and the river tumbled so loudly it might have been a windstorm.

In dreamtime, I sat for hours in the tree and watched the Willamette carry sediment from some other place to the sea. A river is the one thing I know that is always arriving and always leaving, always eroding yet always building. The river carries rain, stone, wood, leaf, an old boot, an empty shampoo bottle. All our hope. All our misdeeds. At once, it holds loss, beauty, sorrow, and renewal. I am learning how to hold all these things, too.

The First Sighting

❖❖❖

I am out before the sun, but a morning glow pours across a line of trees on the Willamette's eastern bank. Splotches of leaves have turned burnt orange and blazing yellow, spreading like a brush fire through the cottonwoods, maples, and ash. Lacy mist weaves its way upriver. With a trail of breath following them, bicyclists in poofy jackets pedal across a nearby bridge. The air coats my lungs with an odd sense of emptiness—the winter ahead and months of low light.

Out here, I sense the air's slouch towards fall and the emptying of summer to a season marked by absence more than anything else. The birds quiet. Trees drop leaves. The land prepares for rest. Today the stillness of the land invites a stillness of mind—a time of reflection and wonder.

❖❖❖

I once took a personality test that claimed it could demystify all my quirks, bad habits, and dreams. It said people like me often fantasize about going back to the past and fixing wrongdoings. I confess I have imagined myself as a time-traveling Wonder Woman who corrects the most horrid of our mistakes. It's something I've done since I was a child. At various times, I've imagined the good advice I would tell Cortes, Columbus, and Cook. Then I would come back to a world overflowing with kindness and good.

I've had a fantasy about the Willamette River too, the river of my childhood. It goes something like this: Armed with the latest studies in stream ecology, I warn the Oregon pioneers about the dangers of filling in side channels and building dams. I show them a map of the current river with its single channel and tell them it doesn't have to be this way. There are choices.

Ridiculous, I know. Because even if the settlers had listened and built their homes and farms away from the river, maybe the story would find a different way to the same conclusion. Or I might return from time traveling and find my own home vanished, since it was built in what used to be the floodplain. Despite the foolishness of my fantasies, I can't help but wonder what it must have been like to see the Willamette Valley as a settler. Imagine the first boats traveling long distances to chart the new land. What did they see and what did they feel while looking at a place unsettled by Europeans?

More than a decade before Lewis and Clark entered Oregon Country, an English explorer named Lt. William Broughton traveled up the Columbia on the *HMS Chatham* and viewed something no white man had ever seen: the mouth of the Willamette River. It was October. Haze knit a white veil over the voyagers' eyes. With his courage tested from living solidly on a wind-tossed ship, and his voice hoarse from yelling orders, Broughton had first faced the mouth of the Columbia, that wily bronco of a river that could buck boats from its back like flies. Two giant basalt walls cradled the Columbia, yet the river's opening hid in the vastness of the sea. Some early explorers mistook it for a major strait and missed the entrance altogether. But Broughton would enter the Columbia, travel farther than any European explorer before him, and see the Willamette River.

The native Kalapuya people may have called a portion of the Willamette, Wal-lamt, which might mean green river. Maybe Broughton saw eddies like giant emerald pendants swirling from bank to bank, or a massive fall run of spawning Chinook salmon, their blushing flanks moving headlong against the current. Did he see, as I have seen, an understory of mist on the water curling toward the sky? Or the yellow torches of fall cottonwoods sending up their flares? Whatever the case, in 1792 Broughton saw a river and surrounding landscape that I might not recognize today.

From journals kept during the voyage, we know Broughton and his crew came across deserted Indian villages and canoes holding the remains of the dead, a kind of sepulchral ritual Broughton and his party did not understand. When they reached the Willamette, Broughton named it the River Mannings, which "commanded a most delightful prospect of the surrounding region."

If I could go back in time to visit Broughton, perhaps I would tell him to look kindly on the river. The water is not just a highway for humans, but a place valued for the sake of its existence, a home for the wild, a refuge for the spirit.

Of course, Broughton was not the first to see the Willamette River. Not even close. The first witnesses were surely animals, and generations of them, since the Willamette River Basin formed over time. Its creation was filled with violence and catastrophe, chunks of earth ripping apart and others smashing together. Thirty-five million years ago a seafloor slab attached itself to the continental margin, ultimately becoming the valley floor. Mountain ranges formed, alluvium filled the valley, and a series of basins developed from the northward movement of the Pacific Plate.

Then, between twelve and eighteen thousand years ago, superfloods of unimaginable speed and power swept into the valley, caused by glacial meltwater that ruptured from ice dams near present-day Missoula, Montana. Meltwater coursed hundreds of miles downstream with flows nearing sixty miles per hour in the Columbia Gorge. To imagine it, picture in less than two weeks' time—the typical length of a flood—more than the *annual* volume of the *entire world's* modern rivers surging through the Columbia corridor. I know. It doesn't help. It's just too hard to imagine. All that water cutting into stone and laying down alluvium time and again created a fertile valley and a river that would attract thousands of settlers.

A few thousand years after the Missoula floods, the first people migrated into the Willamette Valley and saw the river. They were the Kalapuya people, comprising several independent bands connected by language. For more than nine thousand years, the Kalapuya lived with the Willamette and the surrounding land, fashioning tools with bone, wood, and stone, and harvesting plants for food and basketry. Using lines made of willow bark and lures with human hair, they fished for salmon, cutthroat trout, suckers, steelhead, and possibly sturgeon. At Willamette Falls, the Kalapuya fished for an eel-like species called lamprey while trading with other bands. Willamette Falls in particular helped build long-term kinships between tribes, and still does today, says David Lewis, a member of the Confederated Tribes of Grand Ronde and the manager of the Cultural Resources Department.

The Kalapuya were the first human caretakers of the land. For roughly two hundred years, they managed the valley with fire. Historians and anthropologists don't know the frequency or scale of the burns, but periodic fires maintained a prairie habitat that provided food sources such as game, camas, and tarweed. Fire also kept out weeds and competing vegetation. It allowed hazelnuts and acorns to flourish, two other food sources of the Native people.

More than two hundred years after Broughton made his trek on the *HMS Chatham*, thousands of years after the Kalapuya entered the valley, and thousands more after the Willamette was formed, I would get my chance to see this river. At least a side of it I never knew.

A guest lecturer came to one of my graduate classes to speak about the Willamette. He showed us a historical map of the river with a knot of channels tangled upon itself, a complex river unlike the single channel that flowed near my house. I had never seen this river. In school, I had learned about the Trail of Tears, but not the indigenous people removed from their ancestral lands near my home—the Siletz, Yamhill, Clatsop, Tillamook, and Coos. I had learned about the ancient Appalachians but not the Oregon coastals; the Mississippi and Colorado, but not the Willamette and all that had been lost.

Everyone in the graduate class sat calmly, but embarrassment flooded me. How was it that in all my years playing in the water, paddling it, and listening to the lilting songs of the Swainson's thrush, I never knew this story of the river?

I have memories of my sister and myself as young children walking to the river and fantasizing about the fairies living in the St. John's wort and the gnomes in the trees. Another time, in a kind of heroic attempt to win approval from my family, my now-husband, Ben, as a teenager tried his hardest to throw a rock across the mainstem. Despite our cheers and encouragement, he never did. But, man, he came close, which was good enough for me and apparently good enough for my family. But these experiences didn't unearth a realization that so many of the Willamette's channels had vanished—that so much of its ancient wildness was gone. We knew the river had a concerning history of pollution and degradation, yet we didn't understand or know the lingering consequences of simplifying a river. It was a wound we couldn't see.

After looking at the historical map of the Willamette in that graduate class, I began to wonder: Who else has never seen the wild Willamette? And what is the danger of not knowing what a river has lost?

New experiences can seep in quietly like water inching through earth. Or they can strike like a heron spearing its bill into the silver side of a minnow. Seeing a map of the historical Willamette came to me like the heron, setting off a near-frantic search for more information to fill in the incomplete picture I had of the world. As I learned more, new realities surfaced. Things once obscured by half-told truths became clearer, and sometimes muddled once again. "You never step into the same river twice," said Greek philosopher Heraclitus. I rediscovered this simple fact each time I learned something new about the Willamette.

Sometimes I stepped in the water and the cold of it cut like metal's edge. Other times, the water brushed across my calves in a soft kiss. Sometimes the river caught the sky in a near-perfect reflection. Other times, the river dimpled and bent it beyond recognition. How could a single river offer so many things?

In searching for more information, I would learn that in the mid-1800s land surveyors went out in the muck and soppy land to take stock of the Willamette Valley. They trudged through vine maple, hazel, snowberry, ninebark, elderberry, and through crowdings of broadleaf trees. They surveyed the landscape link by link, a link being 0.66 of a foot, the main component of the 100-link surveyor's chain.

The first surveyor maps show majestic ribbons of water hemmed in by the spines of two mountain ranges. The channels formed an intricate lacewing pattern that flowed across a scoop of land. In some places, the river meandered over a width of five miles. The maps also show a river flowing through a wooded forest. These bottomlands, often two miles thick and up to seven at the confluence of major tributaries, contained Oregon ash, alder, black cottonwood, willows, Doug-fir, and bigleaf maples.

With a complex network of sloughs, alcoves, and side channels, the Willamette provided habitat and refuge for many aquatic species. Juvenile fish could rest in the still backwaters. Caddisflies could build their pebble cases without being pummeled. The western pearlshell, a freshwater mussel that can live up to one hundred years, could feed and grow in the shallow secondary channels. Together the main corridor and off-channel areas recharged wetlands and ephemeral streams. They transported sediment and nutrients, and fed riparian vegetation. Overhanging trees offered leaves and wood to the river, providing nutrients and shelter for aquatic animals. It was a complete, beautifully designed web of water, wildlife, and land.

Early settlers and explorers called the Willamette Valley Eden. They spoke of prairie grass so tall that they had to use bells to keep from losing cattle. Others described the land as a swamp with wetlands and

12

ephemeral channels crisscrossing the land. French explorer Gabriel Franchère in 1814 wrote about the Willamette's wooded banks and low swampy fields giving way to hills "rising in an amphitheatre." Peter S. Ogden, a Hudson's Bay Company trader, traveled on the river in 1826 and wrote about a bountiful land ripe for settlement: "A finer stream than the Willamette is not to be found; soil good; wood of all kinds in abundance, roots, elk, deer, salmon and sturgeon abundant; man could reside here and with but little industry enjoy every comfort."

By the time colonizers arrived, Native populations had dwindled. Smallpox first showed up in the late 1700s and returned in subsequent waves. Then what the indigenous people called a "Cold Sick" (likely malaria) spread in the 1830s from Sauvie Island and Fort Vancouver, killing upwards of 90 percent of Native inhabitants in some villages. By the time of settlement, Europeans found the valley virtually unoccupied. From an estimated high of fifteen thousand, Kalapuya numbers had dropped to six hundred by the mid-1800s. Another count in 1841 found only one hundred in the entire valley. No matter the exact number, the Kalapuya people—and many of their traditions dating back thousands of years—fell victim to the settlers' diseases more than their gunpowder. With the demise of Native villages, the burning practices that had shaped the valley for two hundred years stopped. The traders and trappers, mountain men and missionaries had a new land management plan in mind.

With little resistance from the first inhabitants, land was there for the taking—320 acres for a single man and 640 for a married couple. In a ten-year span from 1850 to 1860, the Euro-American population grew from roughly thirteen thousand to fifty-two thousand.

It was time to put the river to work, the settlers decided. Their goal was to concentrate the flow to a single channel so they could move steamboats up and down the Willamette. Beginning in the mid-1800s, the Army Corps of Engineers constructed closing dams built across the mouths of side channels. Downed trees and wood were also used to block the channels. By one account from the U.S. Army Chief of

Engineers in 1875, the settlers saw no purpose for swampy, ephemeral waters that could not move steamships. He described the channel upriver of Corvallis as being "cut up into so many useless sloughs."

Severing channels wasn't enough. The river needed deepening to allow passage of bigger boats, and so dredging began in 1865. Between 1908 and 1929, the Corps dredged an average of 102,000 cubic yards of material each year. This is equivalent to removing more than thirty Olympic-sized swimming pools of sediment every year, the same sediment the river used to build islands and gravel bars, the same sediment the salmon used to spawn.

Excess riverbed material, called dredge spoil, was sometimes deposited where small side channels met the main river, eliminating critical off-channel habitats. The Corps also built wing dams to centralize flow into the middle of the channel. Over time, side channels would fill in or dry out. And of course people wanted to farm, too. They straightened creeks to maximize tillable land. They drained wetlands and filled in the sloughs.

Taken together, these disturbances eliminated miles and miles of river channels. The Upper Willamette (between Eugene and Albany) has undergone the most significant changes. In 1997, scientists Patricia Benner and James Sedell compared 1850s township survey plats, maps produced by the General Land Office, and late 1960s topographic maps, and found that the Upper Willamette has lost between 45 and 50 percent of its original channel miles. A different study found that side channels in particular along this stretch have been reduced from 120 miles in 1850, to 31 miles in 1995, a loss of almost 75 percent.

In addition to eliminating side channels, settlers and agencies such as the Army Corps of Engineers prevented the formation of new ones by stabilizing the bank with riprap (i.e., large rocks). If a settler established his farm near the Willamette, he kept the river from meandering onto his land by fortifying the bank with rocks or snags. Between Eugene and Albany, one quarter of the main channel bank has been stabilized in this way.

The river endured, yet is drastically different. Look at the Willamette today, and that lacewing outline of channels doesn't exist—just the faint suggestion of them in a pattern of meander scars. Small ponds and remnant channels dash the valley, here and there.

Ecologically, scientists know to some degree what this loss means. They know that eliminating side channels is detrimental to fish that need still water to survive. They know filled-in sloughs can no longer store floodwaters and dissipate the river's energy. They know a single channel concentrates the river's power and erodes the streambed to bedrock, where nothing can grow. They know the river has less interaction with the land to bring in nutrients and wood. They know clearing trees from the riverside reduces shade and makes the water too warm for fish.

Yet I wonder if there is another kind of loss that comes from simplifying a river, something deeper, and something the numbers and data can't tell. We cut off channels and in the process our sense of awe of the world, the mystery, the rhythms, and songs of wildness. People of the valley, including me, don't know the power of big floods, or how thick the forests can be, or how the river moves with the tempo of the rain—at least like it used to without the dams.

"One of the penalties of an ecological education is that one lives alone in a world of wounds," writes Aldo Leopold. He's right that knowledge carries a kind of penalty, and in my case, it's brought up a burden of unending questions and contemplation. What does it mean to live with so much loss, with only the remnant essence of something, the soft edges of a place we can only fill in by imagination and not experience? What does it mean for a society to be severed from the ways of a wild river, the habits of places no longer seen? If we don't understand what a river used to be, how can we ever find the courage to hope that it can be that way once more?

It's clear I cannot go back in time and prevent settlers from changing the river. I am no Wonder Woman. How, then, can I live to prevent harm in the future? What does my knowledge of the river's loss ask of me? I am not the first to ask these questions, to wonder about loss or how to live in a world un-whole. Yet such questions need asking again and again so the consequences of our actions don't get buried by time and forgetting, or by the apathy that comes from assigning blame to earlier generations. And even if the questions have been answered, we may not be living fully by the knowledge and wisdom within those answers.

I have sat in my kayak by the wapato and willow of back channels and thought about what all this loss might mean. I've seen stretches of the river choked by large rocks. I've thought about junctures and connections, the rich edges between alcove and main channel, the cottonwoods abandoned by a shrinking water table, the wetlands that once were.

And so here I am now, thinking about the river's wonders and its wounds. The morning light finally arrives and dapples the river's surface. More bikers zip across the bridge, and the mist continues to creep down the hills and settle into the cradle of the riverbed.

It's October, the month when William Broughton first saw the Willamette more than two hundred years ago. It is the time of year when the skies fill with arrows of geese pointing to where they will land. Mayflies crouch under stone. Rain threads its way through leaf, trunk, and stem. Small rodents scurry to dark places, until the sweet grin of spring arrives. The Willamette too will rise and roil over pebble and stone, turning from green to brown like a snake shedding skin. Were the Kalapuyans here in full numbers, they might be harvesting the arrowhead-shaped plant called wapato. They might be preparing for winter, the season of storytelling, when short days and rain keep them inside.

I am also in retreat. Like the land turning towards winter, I am moving inward, becoming still. The robin's song quiets, and so do I. I do not sing but take stock. Listening. Watching. Searching. I read which way the geese point to see where they will land.

Blinking Island
(The Meaning of Change)

❖ ❖ ❖

"Time is a sort of river of passing events, and strong is its current. No sooner is a thing brought to sight than it is swept by and another takes its place, and this too will be swept away." —Marcus Aurelius

Spring

I am late for work and pedaling fast on my bike—past the old railroad tracks and the BMX bike course, pumping hard to make the small climb to the footbridge. I make it up the hill and pass the tree where I once flushed a sharp-shinned hawk. Zipping across the bridge, I look to the right, through the metal railing and out to the Marys River as it weaves into the Willamette. I lurch to a halt and focus on the water. What is that? A flat cap of land is sitting right in the middle of the confluence—an island! I grab the rail for balance and to get a better view. From here it looks like sand, smooth and unrippled. It is small and crescent-shaped, tapering on the upstream end and bending to the river's curve, like a peachy infant tucked against her mother.

I've biked by here almost every day for the last couple of years and had never noticed the island before. Do islands just sprout? Later I would read that islands form in all kinds of ways, sometimes because of high water or at a confluence where the force of one river meets another. And others build up behind a blockage like a fallen log. Some last a few decades, others centuries, which in the scheme of a river is not a long time.

However this island formed and however long it will stay, I marvel that something liquid can create land. And how wonderful to see the island come up in spring, when the world is so focused on newness— robins calling for mates and garter snakes sliding out from dark places. There are seasons in the river too. I wonder what the island will be like in summer when the water pulls back even farther. Maybe killdeer will lay eggs and willows will take root. Maybe it will grow and build a side channel. Maybe shrubs and trees will make a mad dash to colonize the new landform.

I watch for another minute or two, smelling the sweet syrup of cottonwoods and listening to a song sparrow call from a place I can't see. A light spring breeze tussles the trees and carries the song sparrow's tweets and trills across the water. Then I get on my bike and pedal as fast as I can to work.

Summer

Every day I try to look at the island as I zoom past it on my bike, and every day it's the same. Except it's not. Thinking back to how it was in spring, I realize the island has grown. It has risen like leavening bread, spreading out into doughy folds of land. Has it really grown? Or is the water just receding?

One afternoon I shove off in my kayak to visit the island, eager to see the side channel it has created. The familiar smell of wet dying things washes the air, but the river is distant and unfamiliar—swift and deliberate, with dark water hiding the world beneath the surface. Even in July, summer feels like a jagged edge between seasons, unable to decide if it's coming or going, staying for good or just passing through.

At every turn, I flush some winged creature—a kingfisher that voices his annoyance with a clipped rattle. In the willows, a buzzard eating a decaying fish cuts into the air with saw-tooth wings.

The seasons can bring swiftness or sluggishness. Sometimes current brings me to a place sooner than expected, and other times paddling full tilt won't get me there soon enough. Time moves at a different pace on water than on land. Which is why I almost pass the island, sure that I wouldn't get to it for another ten minutes. But ten minutes means something different on a river. This is river time.

Up close, I see the island is not made of sand, but of stones the size of golf balls. On its shore, once-slick algae have hardened into a mucus crust. The rocks are not buff at all. They are the milky blue of an overcast day. At first the island looks barren and sun baked. But when I get out of my kayak to look around, I see small sprigs of willows pushing through. Other things I can't identify are trying to grow. How can something grow through a surface made of stone?

Fall

The island is unrecognizable. I stopped looking at it for a while and it became something different. Bursting with willows. Tangled and messy. Crowded with green. Full and fleshy. Fallen cottonwood leaves speckle its surface. What did it even look like before?

One time on my way home from work, I watched the island from the footbridge. Near the edge, water splattered the reflected moon so carefree that I thought the silver light would splash on the island and take root. And yet another time, fall mist hugged the land so tightly that everything disappeared behind a veil of white. Even within the season, the island changed.

In October, I paddle out to the island to look at it up close. The trip is my goodbye to kayaking for the season and a welcoming of fall. I paddle through the mist until I reach the island. Indeed it has changed. I don't flush out buzzards or kingfishers but instead hear the haunted echo of geese flying above. The island is smaller, its flanks already eaten by the rising water. Leaves of submerged willows flutter near the edge. Shrubs and weeds crowd the rocks, now covered with rain, river, and algae. The stones are no longer milky blue. They are the color of fall—rusty brown, grey, and brick red.

Winter

It is winter. On my way home from work, I stop to look at the island under a crest of moonlight. The night comes so quickly now. The island is gone—swallowed by water or pushed away by torrent flow—and much of the plant life has drowned. All that remain are the bony silhouettes of willow twigs reaching above the swollen river. The stones must be slicked with algae and dead things, or maybe some have been carried off by the high water. The mayfly larvae might be hunched in underwater crevices right now, conserving what they can during winter's low light. I can only imagine from this far away, and under this dark a sky.

Standing out here, the world seems still. The force that grows and tumbles mountains goes unnoticed by my eyes, and yet the world turns, spinning our days and death with the certainty and creativity of moonrise. The fawn lilies burst from the ground and then die, rising and falling like breath. Salmon return to spawn and die in a dance played out for millennia, and underneath the most un-telling of skies, an island blinks out of sight under the Willamette's dark waters.

I watched the island for a year. I saw it emerge from the water, grow, establish plants, and then sink underwater. Who knows what will take its place, or how long it has been rising or falling. At times, the change seemed quick, as if one day the island swelled out into the middle of the channel. Other times, the change seemed imagined, or the island only became something different once I looked away. Fast or slow, the island was in a constant state of becoming, even if that meant becoming nothing. The river seemed indifferent to this becoming—piling up rocks and then raking them away in a blink. Why love or long for anything, then, if it will just be taken away?

Yet there must be some important lesson in loss—like appreciation. But appreciation isn't strong enough a word. *Care* is better. Loss teaches us how to care. Caring that comes from the shared impermanence of all things, from the surge of water and scatter of stones. It is this knowledge—that all things get swept away—that might help us live in deeper awareness.

Change can't be only about the drowning of islands, creation slouching toward an inevitable end, the flicker of things escaping to a dark sky, even if those things help us care and love. Loss is only a part of it. I know this because I saw the island rise, too, and there is more to the world than despair.

The river's same erosive force also brings renewal. A river wears away its banks, but it also accretes, building up stones to create new edges and islands. It floods and wipes things out, but in that process, it also renews life. It builds new channels that have temperatures and flow rates different from the main corridor. And complexity brings an abundance of life. Isn't it a wonder that a single river can be home to microscopic rotifers and seven-foot sturgeon? That it can be so many things and changing all the time? I would call one stretch Place Where Wapato Blooms, another, Tangled Snags, and another, Quiet Green Pool. At a different time of year, I might call these same places Drowned Arrowheads, Washed Out Logjam, and Noisy Brown Pool.

The river creates complexity, and therefore creates. Our own destructive acts might have a side of renewal to them as well. Maybe even in harm we have a chance to rebuild.

Whatever change is about, I fear sometimes we don't notice it—not just how the land changes, but how we change it. We sense time differently than a river. We simplified the Willamette in a hundred and fifty years, which might seem like a long time to a human. After all, it's worth two average lifetimes, several thirty-year careers, and dozens of political terms. But to a river, a hundred and fifty years is just a moment's passing, a geological blink.

I watched an island grow and disappear, but I know there used to be more of these landforms coming and going before so many people were here. Since 1850, total island area has decreased by 80 percent in the section of river between Eugene and Albany. Most of these islands became streamside banks; some truly disappeared and went extinct; and none of the remaining islands are unchanged. Fewer islands mean fewer places for shorebirds to live, or for threatened plants and animals to take refuge.

Chris Maser, a scientist and writer, calls our inability to understand the landscape's incremental changes the invisible present: "Only unusual people can sense, with any degree of precision, the changes that occur over the decades of their lives," he writes. "At this scale of time we tend to think of the world as being in some sort of steady state (with the exception of technology), and we typically underestimate the degree to which change has occurred."

We'll never live as long as a river—that much is clear. But in the relatively short time we have on this planet, we can live with less urgency, until we understand and perceive, and our false senses of disturbance and time allow us to acknowledge what we are losing and what we have gained. Life shouldn't be measured just by its distance but its depth, those quiet places that stir less anxiously, those eddies of the mind that turn and turn again, allowing us to come back around to a place in the world or a place in our mind. Deep places offer a stillness to see beyond our own finality.

I'd like to design an experiment that slows down our minds. Participants would sit all day or a whole week and watch a river. With the stillness of a heron, we would record every leaf fall and wing flutter. We would watch forms shape-shift underneath the surface, taunting our senses and bending our perception of slow and fast. By the study's end, we would see the immensity of changes that happen even in a short period. We might understand the world is longer than our own lives, and perhaps by extension, we could begin to feel the earth move.

❖ ❖ ❖

During the year I watched the island, I spoke to Kim Carson with the Freshwater Trust, a woman with long black hair and crystal blue eyes. She said the most beautiful simple thing about learning to move slowly and appreciate the small and unadorned things of places. She said exactly what I wanted to hear.

> *Just like the river, we have channelized our thinking. And by channelizing our thinking, we lose touch with the subtleties and the complexities of the world; we lose touch with diversity around us; we become too confident, and we move too quickly. It's like the water—if it moves too quickly, it flushes out substrate. We need to slow down and figure out how rivers work. We figure out the river, we figure out ourselves.*

Shards of Beauty in a Fragmented Landscape

❖❖❖

There are at least two ways to get in a kayak. If you have the guts and grace of my husband, you will grab the lip of the cockpit, nose the prow into the water, and kick off into the current with nary a splash. If you are like me, you will read books on how to use your paddle as a balancing device and practice on dry land before hitting the water. And you will still get wet.

I had plenty of practice getting in my kayak the summer we paddled the John Day and Deschutes rivers, Anthony Lakes, and Wallowa Lake. But more than any other place, we paddled the Upper Willamette River. If it was a weekday, I'd watch the clock at work, making sure I wasn't there an unnecessary minute, and dash home so we could do the trip before dark. Once home, we'd gather our gear without saying a word to each other. No time for conversation. Then, we'd throw everything in, make sure our dogs had plenty of water, and whisk out of the house. We could do the ten-mile Peoria to Corvallis stretch in a little under three hours and with enough light to find our way home.

During the first trip on the Willamette that summer, we drove to the put-in at Peoria, accompanied by gentle winds carrying the fluff of cottonwoods like snowdrifts. Summers here are pleasant dreams after a long spell of restless sleep. The rain stops, and people trade wool socks for sandals. They put away long johns, waterproof jackets, and wool hats. During this time of warmth, full of swallows and the chatter of western tanagers, the air carries the distinct essence of the valley: flat fertile fields, and beyond that, tree-stitched hills, ridgeline after ridgeline, and sunsets that lap the sea with an incandescent glow. This flash of beauty charges our batteries for the drudgery of rain and darkness during the rest of the year, and for this reason, no people may appreciate sunshine more than western Oregonians.

No matter how much I hustle to the water, Ben's always in his kayak first. This time, he was doing figure eights in the shallow slack waters of the put-in spot. Meanwhile, I was in the car fumbling with keys, stashing my purse under the seat, and trying to skitter out so Ben couldn't tease me for being slow. My first time back on the Willamette for the season, I had to re-acquaint myself with the water after being away from it for so long. I felt awkward and tippy, and my arms burned as I tried to stay straight and keep up with Ben, who seemed calm as ever picking at his cuticles while waiting for me.

Floating rivers—even open, relatively tame ones like the Willamette—requires reading the water. Not everything can be planned, and what can't requires a mix of reaction and correction, which is likely more intuited than instructed. I'm fascinated by white-water guides who know how many forward strokes it takes to skid around a rock. But even the most practiced paddlers have to rely on split-second reactions. This is an important lesson to remember for a planner like me.

Ben has a natural way of reading a river. He knows to hang on to the outside bank and catch the fast flow—something I had to figure out in a textbook. Sometimes, I'd be huffing and paddling red-faced to keep up, while Ben was letting the river do the work for him. My logical brain, which doesn't shut off even when contradicted, thinks the inside curve is the shortest path, and I'll be damned if it's the slowest.

Once you learn to read a river, you find it has a way of reading you. Personalities float up and become accentuated, in the same way water magnifies stones beneath its surface. The water reflects back your image, but not in exact form. What you see appears dimly familiar, but somehow changed, larger, and fuller than you imagined, and in that regard, a river can show us our essence. I am already prone to lingering; the Willamette brings out my inner slow poke. I love to loiter while paddling. I'm easily distracted by alcoves and islands, sifting through shells and rock by the shore.

If you get on a river enough, the self you've come to know on the water spills into your daily life. Rather than sudden or absolute, the process is like the slow erosion of water cutting a new and un-traveled channel. After many times on the water, I'd find myself watching newly hatched black flies sit still longer than even my usual patience could withstand.

But reading a river sometimes isn't enough. You have to learn the dual art of reading and watching, seeing without looking. You have to sense. You have to learn to keep your head forward and scan for fallen tree trunks but always watch your periphery. If you don't, you risk missing a flash of feather or thrash of a heron—shards of beauty that are more an outcome of patience and perception than actual looking.

❖ ❖ ❖

As Ben and I paddled by Peoria, I noticed the houses—oversized boxes, each with big windows to frame an arresting view of the river. That's all Peoria really is—a few scattered houses. But a hundred and thirty years ago, the town was an altogether different place. Named after a city with the same name in Illinois, Peoria was a bustling port town with four grain houses on the river bank. The river was channelized so steamboats could ship goods. Peoria was at the center of it until the advent of the railway, when Oregon and California Rail bypassed the town in favor of Halsey and Shedd. By 1900, the post office had closed along with Peoria's legacy. Today all that remain are these few scattered houses surrounded by a thin buffer of trees.

27

Downriver a few miles from Peoria, I decided to cut over and take a side channel that I knew connected back to the main corridor. From the far shore Ben maneuvered to follow, then shot ahead. Suddenly we were tucked inside tall walls of red osier dogwood and willows. One hundred and fifty years ago, side channels like these crisscrossed the valley floor. An Army Corps shoal pilot in the late 1800s reported that he had never run the same course twice in two years along a roughly fourteen-mile stretch of the Upper Willamette. Imagine in two years' time still not having seen the full picture of a river. Imagine that many more eagle nests, and beaver, that many more water strider, chub, salmon, and heron. While paddling through the side channel, I wondered: *What did this place look like before settlement?* All I had was this fragment of what the river used to be.

Emerging from the side channel, I saw something flicker by the shore. A brown furry animal slid out of the water and waddled onto the land with a flat paddle tail hitching from side to side. The late sun lit up his honey-brown fur. American Beaver.

Guidebooks will tell you that beaver are common along the Willamette River, but not like they used to be. French Canadian fur trappers and enterprises like the British-backed Hudson's Bay Company nearly killed off these large rodents in the late 1700s and early 1800s, which simplified off-channel areas. When beavers build dams, they backfill channels and create complex features such as pools, which attract rearing fish and osprey. Over-trapping eliminated many of these pools and likely affected other species that use these pools for habitat. Because of their ability to benefit other wildlife, beaver are often referred to as a keystone species.

When you read about the fur industry in Oregon, it's amazing that trappers were able to reduce beaver numbers at all. Trappers mostly worked in the winter, when beaver coats were thickest. This meant they had to wade swift and freezing streams to set traps with a short chain under water. They would anchor the chain to a stake tall enough to stand above the surface, and then smother the stake with castoreum oil from the musk gland of an already-culled beaver. Attracted to the castoreum oil, an unlucky beaver would set off the trigger, get its foot caught in the trap, and then instinctually swim to deep waters seeking shelter. But with the trap's short chain anchored firmly to the stake, the beaver would either drown or die from exhaustion. This method ensured a flawless pelt. Competition was stiff among trapping outfits, so workers would catch all the beaver in the area and leave nothing for rival companies.

I watched the beaver scuttle into a willow thicket before I paddled toward Ben, who had slowed to wait for me. Faster than I could tell him about the incident he said, "I think I just saw a beaver."

"I think I did too."

It was the first time either of us had seen a full-bodied beaver in the wild.

Seeing the unexpected reminded me that the world offers us small gifts through glances, whether a side channel or beaver. These glances, like shards of a broken world, reflect a place and time of wholeness. With enough practice, it becomes difficult to ignore these small bits of beauty, like the white rump of a flicker in flight, or its harsh singular call that knifes its way through the morning air. Glances like the sharp-shinned hawk when it stoops and shows mottled wings, speckled light cast through fir needles, or dew hung like silver jewels on trees. Or mornings just before spring, when sunlight dimples the water and makes the river look metallic, a spray of silver so bright that my eyes water, both from emotion and dazzling light. Or when trees spear new buds into frayed air, even when unexpected cold could snap them back to sleep. Pure gladness moves over my body when the earth pulls back and shows its beauty.

I have seen shards of beauty on the Willamette River when I was convinced it could only offer loss and brokenness. A couple miles downriver from our beaver sighting, Ben and I passed one of my favorite sit spots on a rocky shore. I sat here once in the company of five tundra swans visiting for the winter. At the time, I thought of James Clyman, a mountain man and early explorer of Oregon, who described his Willamette Valley sojourns in a journal. Near the Willamette River, he told of a sky almost blackened by water birds:

> *For miles the air seemed to be darkened with the emmenc flights that arose as I proceeded up the vally the morning being still thier nois was tumultuous and grand the hoarse shrieks of the Heron intermingled with the Symphonic Swan the fine treble of the Brant answered by the strong Bass of the goose with ennumerable shreeking and Quacking of the large and Smaller duck tribe filled every evenue of Surrounding space with nois and reminded one of Some aerial battle as discribed by Milton and all though I had been on the grand pass of waterfowl on the Illinois River it will not begin to bear a comparison with this thier being probably Half a Million in sight at one time and all apparently Screaming & Screeching at once.*

Clyman's time was one of newness and bounty. Lands were wild, and life balanced on a fine point between fate and grace. But even the harsh mountain men, heavy with the trappings of the frontier worldview, were on the receding limb of wildness. In their wandering and pursuit of the unknown, they blazed a trail for the masses to come and alter the lands these rugged individuals had come to understand. Writer William Kittredge witnessed part of this un-wilding. He watched the quieting skies of his southeastern Oregon fields after his family and others had settled and drained the swamplands: "The beloved migratory rafts of waterbirds ... were mostly gone along with their swampland habitat."

I sat for a while on that rocky shore, thinking of Clyman and the Willamette's once-blackened skies of waterfowl, until all five swans took flight at once. Instead of the shrieking clamor of half a million birds, the air carried only the quiet whistle of wings cutting across the sky. Even this was beautiful.

❖❖❖

In the same way our eyes adjust to darkness and begin to discern shapes that were cloaked only moments ago, seeing on the river is a process of slow revelation. After we had seen a beaver emerge from the water, Ben and I kept spotting other wild things. We pulled over to a gravel bar to watch two bald eagles hunting as a team. I've heard this is somewhat rare, since bald eagles are more scavengers than hunters. But they are also opportunists and will hunt if necessary. We watched the eagles flush a swarm of black birds from a row of tall cottonwoods. First, a shifting, dark cloud of wing and beak swarmed the sky, an avian tempest stirred by one eagle. Then there was the thunderclap dive of the other, the clutch of something dark in its grasp, and finally, the dance of feathers circling like a waltz in the silent air. All I could do was gasp at the sight.

What kind of world is this, that offers pieces of dazzling beauty so willingly? That offers gifts even when we dishonor them with destruction? Whatever it is, I'm moved to honor it with gratitude, joy, exaltation, reverence, and—I'll just say it—love.

Some will call it sentimental to love a fragmented world, but I'm okay with that. The word sentimental comes from the Latin root *sentire* (to feel), which is closely related to the word *sense*. Besides meaning perception or feeling, sense has pre-Indo-European roots related to go, travel, or strive after. Being sentimental means searching for the small reminders of what the world once offered—free and wild rivers overflowing with beaver, tundra swans, and eagles. It means we pay attention and watch. It means we feel and sense loss, but also look for the shards of what's left. Living only in loss dams us off from the remaining beauty. For this reason, I am stowing up these shards one at a time. I'll scavenge riverbeds for pieces of shell and rock until I'm worn from searching, until I have a mosaic of the world in wholeness.

On the gravel bar, Ben and I stood as the evening light poured behind the coastal mountains and the eagles went to roost. Near the shore, I trailed my fingers through river rock, and at first, all I felt was stone. But given time, the monotonous swath of stones became all kinds of colors—lavender purple, moss green, and sandy brown. Between rock crevices were small pieces of killdeer egg and broken pearlescent shells.

One by one, I picked up these treasures and showed them to Ben, who smiled at my fascination. I think of my mother, her pockets always full of chipped shells and rocks after visiting the beach. She keeps the best of these treasures in a small bowl on her windowsill.

"You ready?" Ben finally asked softly.

"I guess so," I said, knowing I could stay until dark.

But it was okay because the dogs needed love and we needed dinner—I was content to let this shard of beauty go.

Back on the river, the current whispered against our kayaks. The evening wind roused the trees and brushed against our cheeks. Despite the darkness washing over the river, Ben slowed to meet my pace. We paddled the final mile side-by-side, the twin trails of our kayaks nearly touching.

The Many Truths a River Tells

❖❖❖

On the Water:
Old Eastern Channel, Corvallis, Oregon

The two of us are paddling the Willamette. The earth is dry from the sun's whisper, and a glow that feels not quite like fall casts light on the wings of a thousand midges. It's the end of the day, the time when dark shapes come out and scurry among the deadfall along the shore. Slinky-framed minks crawl hurriedly yet without sound. Then suddenly, twigs snap. Leaves crunch. A towhee scratching leaf litter beneath a dense snarl of shrubs? Or something else?

We sit in our kayaks with the hard plastic hull separating the soft of the water and soft of our thighs. I am concentrating on the feel of water almost on my skin, the river's cool susurrations murmuring against our boats, a sensation felt more deeply with each experience. The first time I kayaked as an adolescent on the Deschutes River in central Oregon, the feeling of being on the water redrew part of the world for me. It became a new way to know a river. I was no longer observer, but participant, and as a participant, I experienced a truth that was before unknown. On the water you become part of the river's course, its pace, and its will. If the river is in a hurry, then so are you. You arrive at the time the current intends, and there is comfort in this.

Since my first time on the water, the picture has been redrawn over and over with the ink of both new and familiar rivers. Each experience became a new line, an unknown channel forming something real. Given time, these threads of experience on the water have become more complex, connecting in a dendritic pattern not unlike a river itself.

Today the river dallies. And being on the water, we accept it. We are kayaking the old eastern channel near Corvallis, which bustled with activity and trade during settlement as the river's once-main course. The channel used to snake upstream of Corvallis in a distinctive "S," with the outside of the upriver curve cutting away each year. Corvallis residents were terrified that the river would cut away to the east and bypass our budding township. This would spell sure death for a river port town with grain mills and landings abutting the water.

To keep the river in place, the Army Corps armored the bank in the late 1800s with wood pylons and rock, called a revetment. River ecologist and historian Patricia Benner told me that you can still see remnants of this historical structure—one of the Army Corps' early attempts to stabilize the bank on the mainstem Willamette. She showed me a picture of the Army Corps installing the revetment. Men with wheelbarrows were hauling material to the site. Even then, the trees near the bank were mostly gone. Patricia showed me another photo of the steamer *Eugene* traveling down this eastern channel in about 1899 with wood pylons from the revetment in the foreground.

I've been tempted to blame the Army Corps and settlers who made this river something so different than what it used to be. But my distaste for this time in history doesn't make it untrue. What is written in the history books cannot be undone. Commerce drove townships. People flocked here with hopes of striking it rich, making a name, and staking a piece of land. Commerce was gospel. Commerce was truth.

Early residents were so afraid of losing the Willamette as a highway that they tried to keep it from meandering. But doing so had big ecological consequences. Revetments impact aquatic life, the flow of the river, and even trees. Cottonwoods especially like to take root on newly exposed soils, yet riprap contains the river's energy, often preventing new gravel bars from forming. Bank armoring sends the river's erosive energy downstream, causing the next landowner to riprap his bank. Sometimes it evens out the speed of the river, which can be harmful to juvenile salmon because they use different rates of flow to rear and feed depending on their size. A bigger fish might use fast water to bring in food that drifts downstream, whereas a smaller fish might not be able to handle the swift current.

So, the revetment was installed and the Willamette never broke away, but in the early 1900s, the river did change course. Eventually, the Willamette formed a new channel, and the eastern branch was no longer the mainstem. Over time, and with less water flowing into it, the eastern channel became a sluggish, narrowed passage.

I tell Ben this story as we struggle to paddle up the lower end of this stagnant stretch. Like always, he responds with imperceptible nods and small *hmmms*. Ben likes to think about things before responding.

We dodge old stumps and logs while shimmying through narrow and overgrown passages. Neither of us can quite believe that mammoth steamboats once navigated these waters. Now the channel is maybe half its former width, with bigleaf maple, red osier dogwood, and willows hunching over the water. With only a band of mallards keeping us company, it feels like we're the only humans to pass through here. For a moment I suspend my knowledge that the old eastern channel has been straight-jacketed and cinched. Just for a moment I let fantasy run barefoot in my mind and pretend we've stumbled upon a place unknown to any other human being. I imagine the river's story as I see it in my mind, the truth before settlement. Giant trees stoop lazily over the water. The river widens and surges while bald eagles fly overhead.

Ben and I are not the first to travel the old eastern channel, of course, which becomes clear when I see crumbling concrete in the water and trash stranded and waterlogged by the shore. Being on the water like this, you see the reality of a river up close, even the reality of our refuse and waste. The eastern channel as a bustling water thoroughfare may not be true anymore, but the mark of humans is still here.

I make a list of every human artifact we come across.

Catalog of Crap I Saw on the Old Eastern Channel:
Abandoned sleeping bag
Floating camping chair
Moss-covered tire
Ice cube tray
Old pipe
Rusted beer cans (and Busch Light, no less!)

Soon we come to an even bigger and more imposing human artifact: the remnants of the revetment project. The wood pylons stand like old bastions of the river, lasting symbols of manifest destiny, the veracity of progress that was etched into most every man's heart at the time. But now, grass grows on top and in the recesses. The pylons are gnarled and hunched, like once-noble guards hardly able to stay above the water. Both of us slow our kayak and look at the pylons in silence.

Seeing the revetment jabs my expectations of what a river should be. I am unable to hold this stillness in front of me.

Ben breaks our silence. "All of this," he says, using his paddle to gesture to the revetment structure, "just shows that we thought the river was ours. We put all this time, money, and resources into making the river how we wanted it. And now it's one hundred years later, and most people hardly know this channel exists. The channel has changed that much in a little over a human lifetime." Ben's right. The reality and story of a river shifts and stirs, depending on the season, the year, or the mindset of surrounding people.

On our way back out the eastern channel, I think about what it will look like in another human lifetime, maybe closing off or becoming the main channel again. Even the pylons, sleeping bag, and Busch Light cans will get swept away by the forces of time. There are a thousand different ways it could play out. Being on the water makes it easier to imagine what the river has been and where it might go, the future reality it might reflect. I think about the next people to visit the channel and how they might feel like the only ones to pass through here. I hope instead of trash and pylons, they believe more fully in the truth of willows and mallards. I hope they enjoy the sinking sun warming their backs.

As on many trips before, Ben and I paddle to our takeout spot. We load dripping kayaks onto the car and pack up life jackets and paddles. The coolness of water will soon leave our skin, the river will wash away any trace of our travels, but we will not leave this place unchanged.

In the Water: Summit Creek, Near Crescent Lake, Oregon

We leave the flattop valley for the mountains. It's just my brother-in-law, Jeff, and me. For miles, Doug-firs, hemlocks, and cedars vault the sky, growing on peaks that seem to have no base. Then moist duff gives way to sandstone and volcanic rock, brittle ponderosa pines and the scent of sage. If the vistas aren't a good enough indicator of the High Cascades, then the feeling of your skin can be. Dryness licks your knuckles, turning them white.

We have come to survey Summit Creek, a small stitch of water at the crest of the Cascade Mountains near Crescent Lake. My brother-in-law reminded me that the Willamette River isn't just the mainstem in the valley—there is a whole network of creeks like Summit in the 12,000-square-mile basin that eventually end up in the Willamette River. We call them by different names, but these creeks are all connected. Why not expand my vantage and explore a creek I had never been to?

For a number of years, Jeff has worked with the Aquatic and Riparian Effectiveness Monitoring Program that sends crews out to survey stream quality, among other things. Interns and vagabonds, naturalists and outdoor addicts mostly in their early twenties come from all over to work for the program, some from Texas, Pennsylvania, Virginia, and Massachusetts. They bring funny accents and stories of strange places, but they share a common love for rivers. Most have never seen Oregon, and some decide to stay once they have experiences with a place that seems to have it all: cold streams, mountains, beaches, wet forests, alpine prairies, skyscrapers, and desert.

On this particular outing, I will spend two days helping a crew map Summit Creek, count pieces of wood in the stream, plot pools and riffles, measure rocks and cobble, collect aquatic insects, survey water temperature and chemistry, and gather a host of other data. I have never interacted with a stream in this way.

When Jeff and I arrive, we gear up from the cab of the Forest Service truck. I put on booties and felt-bottomed boots three sizes too big. The felt will help me stay balanced while walking over slick river rocks. Jeff hands me a box with a net folded in it. "Is this for catching insects?" I ask.

"No, it's to go over your face," he answers. Jeff had warned me about the mosquitoes, but I had no idea how bad they would be. A constant whine stipples the soundscape, and at any given moment several dozen of these bloodsuckers swarm my face. Even in the heat of summer, I wear long pants, a jacket, and gloves as a bug barrier. Any time I lean over and show a crescent of skin on my lower back, a dozen mosquitoes plant themselves and suck hurriedly before I swat them away. By day's end, I will have thirty bites on my lower back alone.

Feeling and looking like a bug-proof Bigfoot, I head down to meet the crew surveying Summit Creek. Turns out they all look like me. The work precludes fashion. I tell the crew how little I know about the science behind streams—one of those things self-conscious people do. Everyone assures me they were just as awkward when they first started. Somehow, their assurance feels more like platitudes, or worse, pity.

The first day I spend learning a new language—the rapid-fire volley of clipped phrases, numbers, and codes. My head swims. After some time, I learn that *L-wet* stands for left wetted edge, *doing fines* means searching for fine particles in a pool, and the word *shadooski* is not a hazing tactic (thankfully), but jargon for an instrument that measures shade.

My first task is to measure rocks at various points along the creek's bankfull width. Bankfull, as the name implies, is when water fills the channel to the top of its banks and begins to overflow onto nearby land.

This is a river's most erosive state. Ironically, flood control dams often keep a river at bankfull longer than under natural conditions—meaning our attempts to minimize a river's power may actually be increasing it.

As I come to find out, bankfull width can be estimated by different indicators, such as a bench or indentation where the water has scoured and eroded the land. Silt from the riverbed may also be present on nearby leaves, left from when the water carried sediment and dispersed it. Vegetation lines aren't always a good indicator, since willows, for example, can grow underwater and within the bankfull width.

My job is to wade across the bankfull width and divide it into five sections. Then I randomly select and measure the length of one stone within each of those five sections. I do this for eleven transects. That means I measure fifty-five different stones. Sometimes I grab boulders or large rocks, other times pebbles only 10 cm across. And sometimes what I grab is too small to measure, such as sand, clay, or duff.

My attempt at playing scientist is full of awkward moments, apologies, and re-dos. I'd lose count and only measure four stones. Or, I would forget the measurements and have to start over.

Luckily, I get to move on. Next I use a net to survey macro-invertebrates, a word that comes from *macro*, meaning large, and *invertebrates*, meaning organisms without backbones. Certain macros like caddisflies, mayflies, and stoneflies can be good indicators of stream quality since they are particularly sensitive to disturbance. Any macros we survey here will be jarred up and sent to a lab for identification and analysis.

Standing above a Tupperware container of our macro-invertebrates, I swat a mosquito whose lifeless body pirouettes into our sample. "You've just contaminated the whole thing," says the crew leader, his face stone cold. *What have I done?* Embarrassment wipes the color from my face. Before I can mutter an apology, he breaks into a smile. "Nah, I'm just kidding," he says, and starts laughing. Being a naïve newbie, I suppose I deserve a little ribbing.

My body relaxes when Jeff tells me we are done for the day. Between the bug bites and constant effort to feign comfort, I am ready for dry clothes and a good meal.

We set up camp along the edge of Crescent Lake. The night is full of card games, bored pauses, and stories of big fish aggrandized by the magnifying lens of memory. The crew members commiserate about a massive stream-surveying site with roiling water. But recalling the experience brings out smiles and laughter. Somehow, our relived experiences play back softer than the first time around. Given time, a river polishes stones, and in the current of our lived narrative, we polish memories. This must be a coping mechanism, so that by our last breath, we are a riverbed of smooth, wonderful memories reflecting light.

One by one, each of the five crew members pulls up a camping chair to face Crescent Lake. Flanking the far shore is Diamond Peak wearing a veil of orange sky. All of us sit and watch the water for a long time without saying anything. Sitting. Staring. Unblinking. I think about the crew members—young people working for low wages, missing families and familiar smells, all to be in Oregon's streams. Not just on them, but *in* them. The world must look different to them, being so close to stream after stream, studying and learning the science of them. Imagine the pathways and channels these people have traveled, and the lessons that different rivers have taught them. How has their sight been changed and complexified? Was this the way to know a river? To study and walk it? To feel the water touching my skin rather than the suggestion of it through a kayak? Was this a river's truth?

Finally, I ask, "What is it about water that calls to humans?"

One crew member, a young woman from Texas with a feather woven in her hair, smiles. In a voice as poetic and soft as a stream, she says water connects all living things. We need it to survive and, at the very least, we can honor it with reverence. Her response isn't unlike that of forester and naturalist Viktor Schauberger, who believed that water was alive and therefore demanded our utmost respect.

The sun splashes across the sky in colors that change with each of my breaths. First marmalade orange, then bruised purple, then layers of color like sandstone. But instead of in the time span of ages, the wind erodes the sky in seconds. Everyone brings out a camera and takes dozens of photos, each one swearing they will take no more—until the sky changes again and becomes something too irresistible to ignore. More photos accompany more stares and sighs. We can't get enough of the moving sky muddled in the lake's reflection. We don't ration or savor its magnificence but drink it in big gulps, trying to find the edge of beauty and discovering there is none.

❖❖❖

The sound of jet skis and motorboats awakes me. *Ugh.* I let sleep douse me again for a bit, until the loud wheeze of a crew member's tent zipper breaks my dream. Not wanting to be the last one up, I stumble out of my tent and prepare for the day.

After a quick breakfast of apple and peanut butter on a bagel, I head back with the crew to Summit Creek, but slightly west of yesterday's site. First I shadow Jeff as he maps the stream channel with a laser rangefinder and electronic compass. The rangefinder shoots a laser beam to determine the distance between two points. Jeff stands with the laser, while another person some distance upstream holds a prism that "catches" the laser beam. The two measure the distance between several points until they have a profile of the stream, including bankfull width, sinuosity (or how much the river curves), slope, etc. The technique allows the crew to "draw" a picture of the stream, one point at a time.

The task is too technical for me, so I join two other crew members who are searching for amphibians and invasive species, as well as measuring shade with the *shadooski*.

Turns out I am pretty good at finding frogs, both Cascades and chorus. During one amphibian sweep, I search the riverside shrubs behind the young woman with a feather in her hair. Sweeping aside a curtain of brush, I see a Cascades frog sitting rock still. "Good eye," she says. "I walked right by him." I smile, both inside and out.

I spend the rest of the day in the stream, knee-deep in water cresting over boulders and slowing in pools. I see insects under water and feel the soft duff and dirt of the land. I touch and feel. The river soaks through my clothes and into my skin. For two whole days, I live *in* a stream, closer to water than I have ever been. I don't see trash and pylons, but bugs and frogs. I am not separated from the water by a kayak but slugging against current, walking over stone, and feeling the water pucker my skin.

When the day is over, all our data, numbers, descriptors, and samples will be sent to different scientists, analyzed, and later churned into a report that gives each stream a score. Points will be plotted. Graphs will be drawn. And conclusions will be made in the passive voice befitting of scientific analysis. But I can't help but feel that the work we are doing, the work these people do all summer long, serves a higher purpose. Between mosquito swats and laughs, we are finding the place where strain meets joy, that transect of two lines coming together and forming a center, a place of truth that was unknown. We are plotting one more point in our vision of the world and learning another way of the river—what it means to be in it. Given time, these points and lines might suggest a pattern, some inferred picture of a stream I have never walked in before, a place unfolding from darkness one felt-bottomed boot-step at a time. I understand it now. Maybe just a little. It's the mystery of the next point, the lines and edges that connect and become something more, that keep these people so close to streams yet so far from home.

Under the Water:
Gravel bar, Upper Willamette and Calapooia rivers

A few weeks ago, I asked my neighbor, Jeremy, to show me how to snorkel a river. Besides living around the corner from me, he is a professional underwater photographer and filmmaker. His nonprofit, Freshwaters Illustrated, has made extraordinary films to teach people about the life, study, and conservation of freshwater ecosystems.

On a warm day in mid-August, when the river becomes shallow and slow moving, I grab my wet suit, which I last used when I was brave enough to surf the Oregon coast, from the closet. I even find my booties and gloves. With our arms draped with snorkeling and photography gear, Jeremy and I head to the river on foot. We run into my parents walking their dog, and then another neighbor who, like me, had heard a flock of geese flying overhead yesterday. Already, yellow cottonwood leaves speckle the trail.

Jeremy shows me how to put on my mask to keep water out. When it fogs up, just wipe a bit of spit on the inside of the lenses, he says. Even though my wetsuit and gloves hug me tightly, I feel a cold shiver upward from my feet when I step into the river—it has been a long time since I last surfed and felt comfortable in cold water. We crouch on our knees to get used to the water. "What would we see if this river was as complex as it was before settlement?" I ask. He says even scientists can only guess. It's a matter of extrapolation. We have pockets of healthy, functioning habitats that serve as references, but it's hard to imagine a whole system as it was historically. I wonder how we can even begin to imagine it without experiencing the river in different ways.

Jeremy suggests we start by crawling against the current very close to the shore. Inch by inch, I submerge myself, and a lip of cold water rings the back of my head. My breath is jagged with sharp inhales until my skin accepts the cold. Sinking underneath moving water is at first both terrifying and satisfying. It might be the closest sensation to flying, but without manipulating or propelling the water, being propelled, passive to a force outside the body. With no sound but rushing water, I can almost sense the curve of the earth reflected from the river's underside.

I have no words to describe what I see. It's so different from anything I have experienced. Underwater, all references recede behind a canvas of wetness. Mountains, grass, and earth become notional, and earth-based metaphors and language turn upside down. Even sound becomes muddled, like sun-warped records. This is not paddling on top of the water, or even walking in it. This is floating under it, fully submerged. In this moment, I am as close to a stream as I can get—under it, down to the gravel bed. Maybe this hard bottom is the place where the truth of all truths reveals itself.

Jeremy points to aquatic insects underwater. Disoriented at first, it takes me several seconds to focus on what he is pointing to. Then huge caddisflies become visible, slugging against rocks in their stone cases as they scrape algae from the surface. Sculpins with fanned fins dart near the riverbed, and small native fish called red-sided shiners swim around my head. Every so often, we emerge from the water so Jeremy can tell me what we're seeing.

"You can see things so much easier than I can," I say. "It's like my eyes don't know what to look for."

"But people who snorkel for the first time often see things that I don't anymore," he says.

I give a half smile, doubtful that I can find anything he hasn't already seen.

After exploring the river by crawling upstream, Jeremy suggests we float to deeper, slower pools to see what we find. That's when he tells me to let go. And if we hold still long enough, he says, the fish might think we are just a log and start swimming with us. I let go, feet first, and watch the world play back in reverse.

I remember the weightlessness, the flashing light rippled by water, the initial panic of letting the current take me. Even the passage of time, which we mark on a daily scale by light, diffuses into something imaginary. No longer segmented by sun and moon, time unfolds in a continuum of current, the unceasing force of gravity moving things downstream.

Aquatic life has developed remarkable adaptations to live in the incessant tug of the river's flow. Some insects have a flattened body to avoid getting swept away in higher velocities. (They call it streamlined for a reason.) Some have suctions, grapples, or secretions to root themselves to stones or other surfaces.

We emerge for a moment. Imagine you are an aquatic insect, Jeremy says. All at once, you must survive and exploit the current, fight it and use it to feed. If you are a black fly larva, you have a silk gland at the base of your abdomen to glue yourself to a rock, and fans near your mouth to catch incoming particles. If you are a net-spinning caddisfly, as a larva you use silk to build a net and catch passing food. And if you are a water penny—an aquatic beetle—you cling to the underside of a rock with your flat, copper, and oval body and use scrapers attached to your legs to remove algae from the surface.

44

I have none of these adaptations, but I reach a place of calm and accept the force of river moving me downstream. Mayflies will do this, too. When they have scraped all the food around them, they sometimes jump into the current and drift to feed.

And so I drift. For once I relinquish control and just float. I don't manipulate, trample, or degrade my surroundings. I have no kayak or measuring instrument. I just am. At last I feel like a participant in this billow of water and light and become, as Jeremy has suggested, a log. A school of small dace swims with me, and one presses its pointed nose against my skin in soft kisses. I smile too big and river water spills in my mouth.

❖❖❖

We move on to snorkel the Calapooia, a tributary of the Willamette River. Jeremy hopes we'll see more here, but the put-in is crowded with people playing and floating. No matter, he says. At least people are getting on the water.

This time I really explore. I find the swiftest riffle and anchor myself in the middle of it, just listening to the sound and feel of water pounding toward the sea. Without Jeremy around to point out things, I find them myself: a sculpin whose spotted body blends in with the streambed's colored pebbles, an inch-long caddisfly case, and then another, and another; tiny, iridescent fish about the length of my thumbnail drift all around.

I try again to describe what I'm seeing and find the words to make the experience known. Please remember this, I say inside. There is no sky but the one reflected through billowing water. The refracted sunlight writhes like an electrical current charging between metal wires, surging through the space opened up by current. Instead of stars, tiny air bubbles spark the water's underside. And remember how quickly everything stirs. But remember the slowness of time, too.

As Jeremy and I are getting out of the water for the last time, I look down and see a water penny beetle on my hand. I likely picked it up while snorkeling a riffle. I almost mistake it for a flake or ovum-shaped pinecone seed. "Oh, it's a water penny," says Jeremy, his voice soft with astonishment. "I've never seen one in this area. Must be one of those things I've grown used to."

❖❖❖

There are experiences that move you closer to a place and make you wonder the meaning of the world, experiences like being on, in, and under the river. So what is the truth of a river, and how many ways are there to know it? Is it a place without humans, something degraded by trash and revetments, something to be studied and analyzed, or something to live alongside, like a log?

I've always been the type of person to search for THE answer, the one path that will lead me straight to irrefutable knowledge. Life is made of iterative steps and there's only one way down the stairs. It's just a matter of peeling back layers until I reach that bedrock of meaning, that hard center of the really real. So I admit I've been tempted to think that floating like a log while touching the streambed is THE path. It's the bottom of the stairs, after all.

Now, I'm not so sure. V. F. Cordova writes that "the story of the mountain people will not be the story of a desert people and their story will differ from those of the lakes . . . and all of them, the stories, will be true." Rivers work this way, too. They are complex. They aren't supposed to be a single channel. They flow many places and reflect back a new world with every stir, constantly re-arranging the pieces and redrawing themselves. This is the practice of rivers.

I am trying to understand this practice and take away the riprap lining the walls of my experience that keep me from moving into a new way of seeing. I am trying to understand the value of complexity, both in our landscapes and state of mind. A new vantage softens the edges of our psyche and connects us in a way more felt than known. The more people experience, the more profound their connection to the world.

Every experience is a transformation because it reflects back meaning that was before unfamiliar.

If you asked me what truth a river tells, I would say something that might have surprised an old version of me. I would say that you might think like a human but you can understand the world like a river. You can realize every experience you have is true. When the world is plural, everything becomes astonishing—a river's flashing silver smile, its depth and darkness, the light reflected on top and underneath, the weight of stones in your hands, and the secrets only a fold of current can keep. You can float the river, study it, or drift quietly in its tug. Each of these ways will be right. And you will never know it all—all the intricacies and pathways—because even the streambed is not a stream's end.

Dread

❖ ❖ ❖

Dread (transitive verb): a: to fear greatly, b (archaic): to regard with awe

Water tumbled over my head. All I remember is the shock of it, not the cold, but knowing that I had fallen in, that I had tipped my kayak and spilt my things in the Willamette. *Dear Mother of God, how will I get to the shore without being swept downriver?* It wasn't a question I asked but felt, my whole body stunned into surviving.

There are times in the middle of the night even now, months after the incident, when I awake in horror. Somehow, I am here sleeping next to my husband and not dead underwater. I am not ashamed to admit that I have thought about what people would have said at my eulogy, what I hoped they wouldn't say—that I was a very cautious girl except for the time I made a big-ass mistake and died.

The mistake started long before I fell in, likely when I got the urge to do a big kayaking trip alone. Ben or a friend had always been there to load the boats and help me read the current. I told people I wanted the freedom and luxury to go out when I wanted, without working around someone's schedule. But looking back at the initial idea to travel alone, I suspect the desire came from a more desperate place, a place not of honesty, but ego. I wanted to prove something to myself and to the world—that I could kayak alone and was strong enough to do it without the help of a man. Rather than start small as a warm-up, I decided to go full throttle and plan an overnight trip.

The Willamette might seem like an unlikely place to make a really bad decision. I had paddled it dozens of times without incident, and each successful outing tricked my nerves into thinking I had this river figured out. It's much tamer than it used to be, and sometimes in late summer near the middle reach, the current moves at a sluggish or even standstill pace. But in other places and at other times, it has a power that today I can hardly ratchet up my nerves to test. But I did test its power on my first solo overnight trip from Irish Bend to Corvallis at a time when the river was supposed to be slow and calm, thanks to the summer's low rainfall and thirteen tightly controlled dams on the tributaries. But there are no "supposed to be's" with a river, and that assumption was my first mistake.

Depending on when you go, the put-in at Irish Bend can be a gravel beach with barbeques and bikini-clad babes. Ben helped me unload the kayak among the clamor of visitors and grill smoke. A man with a wooden boat pulled up next to us and started to un-strap it.

"Ya need help unloading her?" Ben asked the man.

"If ya wouldn't mind," the man replied.

"Ya build her?"

"Sure did."

I've noticed everyone slips into a kind of river tongue by the water, creating a lingual kinship among river folk. "How's it going?" turns into "Howdy." Sentences become clipped and rough-hewn.

After helping the man with the wooden boat, Ben finished unloading my kayak and carried it down to a gravel shore. In my small ten-foot boat, I packed a change of clothes, sleeping bag, therma-rest, guide books, life jacket, whistle, cell phone, journal, binoculars, snorkeling mask, first aid kit, headlamp, bug spray, sunblock, food, water, hard cider, and river maps. After saying goodbye to Ben and the two dogs, I paddled into the afternoon sun. It would only take an hour or so to reach my destination, so I had plenty of sunlight to get there. Or so I thought.

At Irish Bend, steep walls cup the river and farmland runs up to the cliff's lipped edge. Riprap is a familiar sight, but so are side channels and alcoves, osprey and great blue heron. In spots, the river can be swift, bending around elbows of land both highly developed and left alone. The sound of mills and industry rattles the air, a reminder of times when the river was so toxic that fish could hardly breathe. Near the turn of the century, people and industry dumped raw sewage and garbage in the river. People often built their houses facing away from the water. Construction workers were terrified of falling in.

The stretch whispers of something bygone and forgotten, a place just out of reach but still witnessed. Among the noise and development, snags scatter the water like arthritic hands straining to stay above the surface. Each time you go, the river might look different. A gravel bar becomes vegetated, the land shifts, and the hunched-over tree you told yourself to remember next time might have fallen in.

A couple miles in, I took a side channel around Norwood Island. The island is privately owned but undergoing restoration activities thanks to a conservation easement. I had read and researched this channel in my guidebooks. They said the channel could be swift on account of the Long Tom flowing into the Willamette. But beyond mention of the speed, the books gave no other warning.

There are a lot of "shoulds" in this story. Having never been down the channel, I should have scouted it first, even if I had read about it. I should have waited until the river was slower, and maybe I should have gone with someone else.

If I had scouted ahead, I would have seen the massive logjam blocking the channel and buckling an old wooden bridge. But once I saw it, despite the instinct to turn around, I spotted a small opening and thought I could get through. If I were a better paddler, I would have gone for it. But it was soon obvious that my beamy little boat couldn't fit through the clutch of branch and wood. If I were braver, I would have finessed my way through the obstacle course and made it to the other side. But I did not scout, I was not a better paddler, and I was not brave. Before too long, I was caught in a tangle of current and flow, trying to negotiate the mighty gravity tugging the river downstream, and the friction of water hitting branches that scattered the river in all directions.

When I realized I would run into the logjam, I turned my boat so it would hit broadside. Just before impact, I leaned toward the jam to grab a branch so the water suctioning under the logs wouldn't flip me over. A hollow thud sounded as my boat rammed into wood. *This is it*, I thought. *This is how people die on rivers.* Logs or fallen branches suck you under until you're caught in swirling water and drown.

I've heard the best thing to do if you get knocked out of your boat is dive down to get out of the suction, but this presumes there are no other branches or obstacles below that might quicken your death. The other option (if you know you're going to hit the strainer) is to swim toward the object with all your might and heave your entire body over it so you get kicked downriver. I did neither. I was still in my kayak, grasping a branch while gritting my teeth.

With my kayak parallel to the length of the log and stern pointing river right, I used the branch to heave myself backwards toward the shore. Then when my arms were extended forward as far as they could go, I would quickly release, grab hold of another branch, and move the rear of the boat another foot toward the right shore, all while fighting the suction trying to flip my kayak. It seemed like forever, but the water calmed. Then I spun the nose of my boat a quarter turn and paddled against the current as hard as I could (stoke-stroke-stroke-stroke), determined not to the let the water sweep me downriver and back to the logjam.

I should have read the online guidebook about Norwood Island that said paddling upstream in this channel is difficult, if not impossible. The current looked swift going in and felt even swifter paddling against it. I zigzagged across the channel to avoid logs and fallen limbs and stuck with the slower flow on the river's inside bend. My progress was slow and painful. My arms burned, sweat broke out on my forehead, my heart thudded against my fear-struck rib cage. Before the fastest part, I pulled over to the bank and rested in a rootwad so I could plot my way out. It didn't look good. The nearby bank was tall and steep, so portaging my boat seemed impossible. Looking to the river, I couldn't see any smooth sections that might help me across this conveyor belt of water. I would just have to paddle upstream with my muscles and will at full tilt, which, in the end, wasn't enough. Despite grunting, paddling, praying, pleading, and thrusting my body forward in time with my paddle strokes, I couldn't reach the main channel and had run out of steam.

Under the fold of some brain lobe, my synapses made an executive decision and I quit paddling. In an instant, the water spun my kayak around and shot me downstream, back toward the rootwad where I had rested minutes before. My kayak hit a small fallen log broadside and flipped over. Cold water. Wide eyes. Sharp gasps. Somehow I grabbed onto the gunwales of my overturned boat and swam to the rootwad. Somehow I kept my paddle, backpack, sleeping bag, food, and even the hat on my head.

With my boat wedged into the gnarled hands of a cottonwood and gear safely stowed in the cockpit, I knelt in the river mud and wept. The reality hit like a cold punch to the gut: My cell phone didn't have reception. I was alone and drenched. I needed to get past sixty feet of swift upstream current to get back on the mainstem.

Wiping away tears and gritting my teeth, I looked to see how I could get up the seven-foot bank. The once-impossible became my only option. I was going to portage my boat, which meant lifting it over a sheer edge crawling with Himalayan blackberries. A small section of the shore was packed with a mound of muddy sediment, forming a two-foot shelf that could give me some height to hoist myself onto the bank. But I figured I could only step on it once or twice before it crumbled against my weight and washed into the water. After that, I might not have a way to get on land. There were no nearby branches to grab, and the bank would be too tall to climb without the mud mantle. Later I read online: "portaging this stretch is inconvenient."

Inconvenient is about the nicest way you could put it.

First, I tied my boat up, hoisted myself onto the bank, and scouted ahead. That was one use of the mud shelf. It had better be worth it. Though thick and tangled with blackberries, the bank had a small clearing that would allow me to walk through and get around the swiftest part of the side channel current.

Back at the rootwad, I emptied my kayak to make it light enough to hoist ashore. From some unknown and secret place of strength, I threw my gear and lifted the boat onto the bank without spilling anything, even though my arms were weak from paddling. Then, I stepped on the mud shelf again to climb the bank, and from the edge, I watched the sediment sink and sift into the water. Then I stuffed my kayak with gear, slung a backpack over my shoulder, and pushed through the blackberries about twenty feet closer to the mainstem Willamette.

Muddy, sweat-soaked, and trembling, I slid my kayak down the steep bank and back into the side channel. *Just forty more feet of paddling upstream. Then I'll be back on the mainstem again.*

I paddled hard. I could see the flow of the mainstem Willamette and began to rattle a silent prayer. *I promise that I will pray more.* Forty feet turned to thirty. *I know I don't go to church anymore but maybe I'll start.* Thirty feet became twenty. *I know I'm selfish and swear too much.* Twenty feet became ten. On the last stretch out from the side channel, a willow branch snagged the sunglasses off the top of my head. "I don't give a shit! You can have them!" I said aloud. I'm not sure if I was talking to God, or to the river.

❖❖❖

I arrived two hours later than expected at my overnight destination—a small island within a greenway parcel called Sam Daws Landing. The turn of the Earth was pulling the sun down fast. I took out my wet things and hoped the remaining light would dry them. Small gravel bars and willows sat cloaked against a sky the color of something I wanted to drink. Behind me, a small channel meandered, and beyond that, a fortress of cottonwoods harbored a group of juvenile bald eagles. For a moment I thought they were golden eagles, since one has been reportedly sighted here, but then I heard their call, which registered between a staccato horse neigh and a maniacal monkey.

Trudging around, I flushed out a fawn still with its spots. Beaver and white-tailed deer tracks pitted the soft earth of the shore. For what felt like hours, I sat and watched clouds slide across the now-pale sky. Such a place pulls you into a center you swear you knew once, maybe not actually, but in a dream.

There's a feeling that comes after surviving danger—a flutter in the heart, an almost imperceptible weakness in the knees, and a careful step. But that's not all. If it were, nobody would ever go out to wild places or face the unexpected. Along with the sinking feeling in your gut—that you just cheated death—is also the rise of something so primal and childlike, so unfiltered and unprocessed. After danger you will notice the feeling of wind trilling your skin; maybe you will smile at the soft drumbeat of your heart. The feeling reaches deep inside, resting in the momentary awareness of being alive. It was there with me on that island.

As my body shook, all I could think of was the texture of my grandmother's hands, like *papier-mâché*, and I suddenly wanted to hear her raspy voice sing every song she knew. Then I imagined Ben mummied tightly in a thin sheet getting ready for bed, the way he sleeps in the summer. I wanted to listen to my dad talk about the birds he saw that day, without distraction or thinking about all the work I had to do.

Experiencing the world in wildness made the echoes of my relationships clearer. It was as though I saw ripples in water, but also found the stone that made them. In surviving danger, we come back around to the people and places that make us whole—like concentric circles connecting beginning and end, forming a new but somehow familiar tale of a hero whose narrative resembles our own, a narrative of going out alone, facing danger, crossing thresholds, and coming back transformed.

Ask me what I think about danger, and I will tell you it can be something good, not wholly, but partially good. I say this even knowing that restoring and reconnecting some of the Willamette's channels could increase its wildness and even danger. I would not have believed the goodness in danger before going out alone. Let me get something straight: I would *never* knowingly risk my life on the Willamette again. But after facing danger first-hand, I have been able to understand the complexity of what it means. The menacing unexpected is not just about fear and horror, but an acknowledgement that existence itself is sacred.

That night, I slept in a depression of grass I imagined a deer had made. Throughout the hours of darkness, a great horned owl called in a song I could not decipher. I was content to just listen and not tax my brain with the meaning of it. Sleep came like a slow descent. Each breath carried the power of two dissonant emotions with a single name—a simultaneous sinking and rising, an emptiness and fullness. Together, the weight and lightness resonated inside, then up towards the sky. And the sky! Somehow it held both a darkness and shine. The blackness above faded to an iridescent glow, with the hills beyond rimmed by a line of glorious blue.

Memory

❖❖❖

The computer at my work desk flickers on, casting a blue glow across my hands. I have come in to work early to see what an Alzheimer's brain looks like. My grandfather is dying from the disease, and I want to know what is happening to his mind. I type in "Alzheimer's" and search for images. The pictures haunt me.

One image shows a slice of a healthy brain next to one with advanced Alzheimer's. The normal brain is peachy and ringed with curving folds, a river delta. In comparison, the Alzheimer's brain is shriveled and hollow. Dark spots and holes puncture the lobes. The absence. In the Alzheimer's brain, the thick pink folds of the healthy brain have become gnarled, garish stubs—stunted, withered, and shrunken. Channels of dendrites and axons have been severed from the neurons and dissolve into obscure hazy clouds.

Saved on my desktop is a digital copy of a Willamette River map that has become a central image in my research: the river in 1854 next to the same river in 1975. In the 1854 map, channels meander their way across the valley floor. They curl, arch, fold, and coil to create a unique pattern. Channels extend outward or loop together to form islands. The

1975 map shows the same river, but it's shriveled and disconnected. Tiny dashes show the faint suggestion of where river once moved across the land in dazzling sweeps. The absence of channels isn't like dark holes. It is marked by the glaring white of the page. So much page, so little river.

While staring at the image comparing the Alzheimer's brain to a healthy one, I read an accompanying article. It says our experiences create patterns in the types of signals zipping through the brain. These unique patterns are how the mind codes our memories and sense of who we are. Alzheimer's tissue has fewer nerve cells and synapses than a normal brain. Over time, nutrients and other essential supplies can no longer move through the cells, and the cells die.

Alzheimer's literally simplifies the mind. My grandfather's self is dying.

I get up, shut the door to my office, and quietly cry.

❖❖❖

Grandpa had been falling. Sometimes he'd be taking a walk and suddenly lose his balance. We'd all assumed his legs were getting old. But it wasn't just age, we found out.

"Grandpa has Alzheimer's," my mother said, sitting at her kitchen table, her head lowering, as if to tell a secret. Apparently, during a routine checkup at his hospital in Florida, my mother's father had wandered off and became disoriented, soon frightened, and realized he didn't know where he was or why he had left his home in the first place.

How could it be? Grandpa had danced at my cousin's wedding a year ago. He had just visited from Florida to attend my brother's high school graduation, smiling in praise like everyone else.

Days later, I called the local chapter of the Alzheimer's Association and asked a woman to tell me, in the simplest terms, what causes it.

"We're living too long," she said.

"Oh I see." I quietly thanked her before hanging up.

How cruel of the world to take away a person's memories. All those pathways carved into my grandfather's brain by people and places, all those experiences nestled into neurons, all the stories, lessons, and memories, taken away. Do the channels of the brain really disappear? What happens when you can't recall an experience anymore? Do you unlearn a lesson? Do you un-become yourself?

My grandfather's disease is even more mysterious because I don't know much about his life and the experiences that anchored his memories in the first place. I can count on two hands how many times I've seen him: he's always lived in Illinois or Florida, which means I've had to thread stories together into a makeshift map of who he is. His lifeline isn't always straight in my head. The dates are often wrong, and important events of his life come in chaotically, like tributaries entering a stream. I've collected impressions of him, two-dimensional artifacts, piecing him together from stories told and retold, from old photographs of a tall, handsome man with a dazzling smile, crisp blue eyes, and swept-back brown hair.

I know he grew up poor. His father was a stern minister who didn't believe in medicine, only God's power to heal. My grandfather watched his mother suffer from diabetes and die from gangrene because she wasn't allowed to get hospital care. Then, my grandpa learned a harsh lesson in hypocrisy when the minister himself checked into a hospital to cure a bout of tuberculosis. Mom said that, when she was growing up, she and the whole family went to church, except for Grandpa. He stayed home.

He was an executive at Caterpillar Tractors, selling big earthmovers. I wonder what he would think of me, rallying to restore a river. If I dug beneath the surface and got to the heart of the man, would I even like him? Would he like me? He may not be pleased to know that I love *The Monkey Wrench Gang* (if he's familiar with the book at all), or he might not care that his big tractors, which once filled in waterways everywhere, are now being used to rebuild rivers like the Willamette.

There are things about a person you can't discover from photos and stories, like the many ways he laughs and all the things he loves, the pitch of his voice when he's excited or sad, the softness in his blue eyes when he apologizes, or what places in the world make his heart quiver. These things I can only guess about, and now he is forgetting them, too.

❖❖❖

When my grandfather's disease was really bad, I found needed distraction in my research on the Willamette. Often I'd look at an old photograph and daydream about the historical river, wishing deeply I could transport myself to the wild Willamette and know it viscerally.

One image I've looked at many times is a late-1800s stereo-card called *Trouting on the Willamette River, Oregon*. The image shows a wall of fir trees with speared tops in the distance, and two men in the foreground fishing in the shallow waters. You can't see their faces. But I picture them with harsh blue eyes, thick brown hair swept under a sun hat, standing tall and lanky among the gravel bars and islands. Next to them, roots from fallen trees snarl the shore. The river splits and then rejoins, flowing around vegetation and creating a network of channels. In essence, it's complex and messy.

Images like this stereo-card are all we have of what this river used to be, the scraps of other people's experience. All we have is the second-hand telling of history, and I've strung it together into an interpretation that may or may not be true. No matter how long I look at this photo, I can't hear the sounds the men heard while fishing, the sweeping gurgle and wash of water around tree trunks. I cannot see the flashing silver blades of trout cutting through current, or smell the tangy scent of broken fern mixed with baked summer earth.

When I read about the Willamette's four-fold decrease of river shoreline, I imagine all that complexity and all those seams between earth and river unraveling bit by bit. Where did all that river go?

Some of it has dried up, and some of it goes to our homes and to the fields. Gas-powered pumps pull river water into pipes that feed irrigation sprayers. The water sprays into the air from a million jets and dissolves into hazy clouds. I have seen rainbows in those clouds, scatters of light caught in the river's prism and lifting to wind. From above, they might look like sprays of color hovering over places where river once flowed, remembering disjointed channels and bends.

❖ ❖ ❖

My mother is sitting cross-legged on the couch, surrounded by junk mail, old calendars, and random bills and bank statements to sort through. I tell her I want to talk about Grandpa, because I don't understand what is going on. His disease feels far away and unknowable, my grief distant and unfocused, like trying to learn the grooved contours of his life through another's blurry lens.

But it is chaos in their living room. My sister has come over and is talking about her new house. My dad is trying to show me the differences between pintails, teals, ring-necked ducks, and northern shovelers. My mother recounts a nonsensical conversation she had with Grandpa over Christmas. It went something like this:

"Hi Dad."

"Thank you, honey. Oh thank you, honey."

"Oh that's nice, dad."

"Thank you, honey, oh thank you, honey. Thank you, honey. "

"All right Dad, well, I better go."

"Thank you, honey, oh thank you, honey . . ."

Midway into the story, my mother mutters something to herself: "I don't know why these people keep sending me return address stickers."

I have so many questions. Is Grandpa really bad? Can he talk normally? Does he think? Does he tell stories? As soon as I start to ask one question, my dad calls me to the computer to show me pictures he took of northern shovelers, with their spade noses.

I sit back down. "Mom, do you know what is going on in his brain? What it looks like?"

She pauses. "I don't really know."

Then she looks down at a piece of mail from Doctors without Borders. "Do you have any need for a map of the United States?"

❖ ❖ ❖

In the beginning, we didn't hear much about my grandfather's Alzheimer's. I'd check in once in a while, and Mom said he was doing fine, or that his medication and therapy had slowed the progression. She visited Grandpa before he was put in a home, and, during one conversation, he referred to his wife—my step-grandmother Eileen—as "that woman in the kitchen." The woman he had called his soul mate had become a nameless face, just like that.

It seemed if we turned our heads away for even a moment we'd find slight but troubling changes in his mind when we looked back. He'd forget names and get confused in unfamiliar places. He was mostly whole—mostly Grandpa—but bit by bit, he began to change as the geography of his mind withered.

"Did you tell Grandma Eileen that he forgot her name?" I asked Mom.

"No," she said, squinting her eyes, not in a grimace, but almost. Even though I wanted to, I didn't ask anything more about it.

During another visit, Mom said Grandpa told vivid World War II stories, and he recalled the names and ranks of all his fellow fighters. This surprised everyone because he has never talked about the war before. He told my mother a story of how he almost crashed his plane coming down from cloud cover. My grandfather realized he was dangerously close to nose-diving into the ground. If it hadn't been for the hands of some unknown force, he insisted, he would have died. This also surprises us, since he has never been a religious man.

More and more, his eyes glaze over in confusion as he is talking to my mother, and it's clear he doesn't know who she is. My mother tells me this at her kitchen table, the same table where she first told me that Grandpa had Alzheimer's. Inside I am appalled, thinking what it must feel like to be erased from your father's mind, to be an abandoned, hollow spot. Imagine seeing that momentary flicker of doubt in his eyes, his scared expression saying, *I don't know who you are.* It must have feel like sudden erosion, a once-stable bank slipping away.

"Do you feel like you've lost your father, even though he's still alive?" I ask. My face is still, but inside, I am begging for a tender moment with my mom.

"Yeah I do," she says, matter-of-factly. She continues to set the table for dinner, her eyes looking down on each napkin she folds. Then, she looks up at me. "He's not the dad I knew."

❖❖❖

By now, the two men in the stereo-card are long dead, and the riverbank they explored might be buried. Maybe it's a gravel pit or the view from someone's home. The looming firs have been cut down, and the trout don't flash as brightly, with fewer of them swimming through the current. Academics debate how and when the Willamette lost its channels. Some think it happened mostly during settlement, while others say channel loss occurred more dramatically as agriculture expanded in the mid-twentieth century.

When you compare a historical map to a current one, it looks as though the channels dried up and vanished one day. But it happened slowly, one closing dam at a time, until the two men turned their heads and saw the place they always fished had been altered. Perhaps they were troubled to see slight changes to the river. But maybe they weren't. In the 1930s, Oregon constituents rallied for federal aid to prevent flooding and maximize the land for productivity. In response to public and industry demand, the Willamette Valley Project Committee was formed, with the lofty goal of building high dams to keep the river in check, though the dams would also impact salmon runs and keep the Willamette from flowing into its usual channels, among other consequences. William L. Finley, a nationally known naturalist, was the only individual who "spoke out early and often against the building of high dams on the Willamette drainage."

One voice was not enough. Willamette Valley citizens wanted flood control to protect their assets and infrastructure. The Army Corps and supporters of the committee had their way, and the first two dams were installed in the 1940s. The majority of the dams were installed after the floods of '43 and '45 (two years of devastating high water) and during the post-World War II economic boom. Today we have thirteen federal dams within the Willamette Basin, plus a whole scattering of smaller ones on private land.

As a result, over time the Willamette has behaved differently in its rhythm and patterns—no longer meandering where it used to and abandoning places it shaped long ago. Historically, the river had peak flows around February, and maybe also in April or May. Today, the frequency and intensity of peak flows have been reduced, with reservoirs dampening them by 30 to 50 percent.

Sometimes I wonder if the two men in the stereo-card even noticed the Willamette changing. Maybe they forgot, from year to year, how the river used to flow and flood. Does the river forget, too? How much can a river lose before it isn't itself anymore?

During the chaos of trying to learn more about my grandfather's disease and piece together his life, I find a journal I had kept as a fourteen-year-old. I don't know what compels me to read it, since I haven't looked at it in more than a decade. Maybe a subconscious urge to understand my own memories moves me. The power of keeping record has become imperative, even though memories are a poor substitute for first-hand witness, and even though they are vulnerable to error, exaggeration, and complete unraveling. Sometimes, they are all a person has.

My journal as a fourteen-year-old has a fairy on the cover, surrounded by a purple border. In between heartthrob dispatches about loves that never were, I wrote about the Willamette River flooding in 1996, the only experience I've had of a true flood. "The roads have changed so much!" I wrote. "They are no longer roads, they are rivers. Now the whole city is covered in thigh-high water . . . and we're in a state of emergency."

Reading this, I recall the winter of late snow and the heavy rains that followed. I recall the roiling brown waters, my mother and I huddled in coats, walking to Willamette Park to see the high river. We stood still for minutes in awe of the drowned parking lot. I recall people floating in canoes near my home. My family was unable to get to town and had no working phone for three days. For three days, the world stopped, or at least moved a little slower. Everything normal, like school and friends, was suspended, and our family entered a time of closeness, brought together by a restored wonder in the world—bonded by the knowledge that a river under the tight grip of humans could still flood.

Years later, while volunteering to help paddle elementary students down the Willamette, I saw an aerial photograph of the flood. Before we hit the water, parents, teachers, guides, and students circled around an aerial photo of the flooded Willamette, showing brown water filling in dead sloughs and disintegrated channels. We saw the river transformed from a single pathway to dendritic channels branching into places that no longer existed on current maps. Channels charged and pulsed across fields and around homes, reaching into and reconnecting forgotten streambeds. I stretched my hand across the image, and the river meandered beyond the length of my fingers and palm. Then I did the same to a historical river map blown up roughly to scale, and my hand stretched about the same distance. The river in 1996 became nearly as wide as it once was. Though people seem to have forgotten how the Willamette once looked, the river has not forgotten. At least not yet.

This is how I learned that rivers have memories—ancient memories surface again and again through flooding. Despite dams and irrigation sprayers and filled-in fishing holes, the river still finds its channels. It still remembers.

The Willamette has flooded many times. In 1881, a flood destroyed all the fall wheat on the Long Tom valley. Bridges were taken out or relocated. Scattered in old news clippings are tales of families escaping the high waters. One story tells of a family by the name of Ash, who were living in the woods when the high waters came. It drove them from their home at 2 a.m. Grabbing lumber and nails, Mr. Ash built a tree fort for shelter. As the waters rose, he built higher and higher, until another family came to the rescue, paddling the floodwaters with oars "made from rails." Altogether, the Ash family were stuck in their makeshift tree fort for twenty-nine hours.

In the flood of 1943, at least nine people lost their lives, and hundreds were reported homeless In 1964, some seventeen thousand were made homeless, and the old-timers in Junction City, even those accustomed to floods, were amazed at the "new river" running through the town.

Time and again, the Willamette River has flooded, reconditioning its channels, forming and reforming its patterns. Human memory is encoded in the same way, written by the initial experience but reinforced and changed through recall—memory is not quite like perception or imagination, not quite real or based in fact, yet it influences reality all the same. Both rivers and humans re-write themselves through time, with long-gone realities continuing to shape the present. Yet where humans forget and succumb to error, dementia, age, brain-shrinking Alzheimer's, and cloudy confusion, rivers have the advantage of floods—those cleansing waters that come again and again, that expanse of river, the freshet that redraws the pattern and makes things whole again.

❖❖❖

The phone rings. It's my dad. He gives me an update on Grandpa.

Grandpa can't even talk. He plays with crayons and has his diapers changed like an infant. His wife becomes his mother sometimes. His own mind denies access to places he grooved long ago.

Days later, or maybe weeks, my mother writes to me in an email: "Papa and I have decided to go to Tampa to see Dad & Eileen." I read it while getting ready for work. I stop eating my toast. "He is not doing well, and it's time for us to go. One thing I want to take is stories about Dad that I can tell him while I'm there, even if he can't understand or respond much. So, do you have a story or two I can share?"

I read the message and then wipe away a few tears. I don't have any powerful story to share. All I have of my grandfather are faint memories. I remember him coming to visit when my mother was about to give birth to my brother. I came home from school and there was a tall man with white hair in the kitchen. I remember telling him, that same visit, that I wanted a pair of red high heels. Instead of lecturing me that five-year-olds shouldn't wear high heels, he let me fantasize. I remember going into my parents' room in the morning with my sister and seeing my grandpa and Eileen instead of my parents. They told us my mom had given birth to my brother in the middle of the night. My sister and I jumped and screamed in excitement. Small stories like these are all I have.

Writer and environmentalist Freeman House says, "In one ancient language, the word *memory* derives from a word meaning mindful, in another from a word to describe a witness, in yet another it means, at root, to grieve. To witness mindfully is to grieve for what has been lost." Memories are not just about nostalgia or sharing a good story. They are testaments of things lost, of places no longer wild, and of people no longer whole.

How did I let it happen this way? Our elders are supposed to teach us wisdom. Why else do we live for decades after our childbearing years? From a pure biological stance, we serve no purpose once we can no longer pass on our genetic imprint, but culturally we do. My grandfather's channels of experience were once deeper and more expansive than mine, but I will never get to walk them. I have no stories of sitting on his lap, listening to his resonant voice tell me how the world works. He only exists through other people's memory, and the faintest outlines of my own.

❖ ❖ ❖

Just before my parents leave to say goodbye to Grandpa, I take a walk to the river with Ben and the dogs, but we don't get far. The path is a river channel. The water has flooded and now trills quietly. We watch the water sift and stir around the trunks of submerged trees. The white alders dangle their seedpods, almost in an offering to the riverbed. A father and mother with two small boys come to see the water. The dad is explaining what happens when it rains and rains and rains. It floods, he says. He doesn't say it with malice, just acceptance. One boy comments that they should get a vacuum cleaner and suck up all that extra water. Ben and I turn toward each other and laugh.

Ben climbs an algae-slick log to see how far back the water flows. It's a long way, he says. The water goes farther back than either of us can see.

I used to picture my grandfather's memories rising into the ether, scattering like a faded winter song. But now, I picture them drying in the glassy backwaters of a river, sinking softly underground, into the mud of the world and into all that has ever been.

Far away from here, beyond the time when my grandfather's brain and bones will soften to river grit, the Willamette will keep on flooding and re-*membering* itself, connecting to its ancient kin of channels. The story is not the same for my grandfather. His essence will drain and ebb into hazy clouds that carry only the suggestion of places his mind once meandered. The dendrites will dry, the space between them unable to hold the pattern of the man I had hoped to know.

There will be no flood to bring him back.

Story Mapping

❖❖❖

"The universe is made of stories, not of atoms," says poet Muriel Rukeyser. If she is right, then stories form complex narrative compounds that build our bones and skin, combining in odd and wondrous ways as we grow. Around campfires and dinner tables, between two friends, and in the tight circles of teenagers, people share the essence of their lives—the communion of experience fundamental to our existence.

Stories of the land fascinate me because they reveal the intricate tangle between humans and the places they live, the topography of both earth and storyteller. I wonder what tales rest in the soft mud by the Willamette's banks, what bits of narrative would waft up like molecules if I pressed my palms into the wet stones of a gravel bar. What does the Willamette River look like in story form, a great tome written by thousands of people, told over thousands of years?

One Kalapuya story tells of a man who lay down in an alder grove and "dreamed his farthest dream." He dreamed of his lands taken over by white men: "the white men came," the prophecy reads, "...and we knew we would enter their dream of the earth plowed black forever."

The Kalapuya prophecy was right. The white man came, and Oregon's story changed. There were unforeseen consequences of the earth plowed "black forever," stories of pollution, chemicals, dried up backchannels, and fields stripped of their rich soil. It's easy to vilify the farmer, but there are also stories about those trying to put it back, and those who see domestication as an advancement and sacred responsibility.

Despite the common narrative of landowners exploiting the river, I searched out people invested in the river's health, because I wanted to learn about how the Willamette used to look, how it changed over the years, and how it might look in the future. I wanted to hear about the cleansing floods that swept the valley floor or reclaimed a slough, or about the channels that still meander in the minds of people by the river. Taken together, tales of our landscapes are like moving maps, shifting through time and showing us the world in its past, present, and possible forms. They are perhaps more powerful than traditional maps that illustrate a fixed point in time, because stories show the Earth's changing geography and the people who are part of that place.

What follows are stories of a few farmers and landowners who are helping to restore the Willamette's complexity. I share them in hopes that they redraw a map of the river, a place deeper than our current experiences can take us. I can't promise that all these yarns are straight and true. In the same way that maps distort continents, stories bend reality. Interpretation is the right of the mapmaker. This chapter honors that truth.

Gary and Steve Horning
Deerhaven Farms, Monroe

Gary and Steve Horning, the father and son team of Deerhaven Farms, know a lot about the Willamette River, their family having farmed next to it since the early 1900s. On an overcast but dry day in November, they agree to talk to me about their family's history with the river. Both father and son are tan despite the sun's weeks-long absence. Both wear green button-up shirts. And both hold a steady eye while talking, the mark of someone knowledgeable about the subject at hand.

On his mother's side, the family moved to an area along the Upper Willamette called Harkins Lake around 1910. The other side of the family came into farming a generation later. Gary's father first bought property down on the river as a teenager before serving in World War II. When he returned, around 1945, he followed a simple edict from the Unites States government: clear the land and feed the world. So Gary's father cleared the thick brush with dynamite so he could start the farm, taking off only Christmas and Easter.

Gary's grandfather remembered when the Willamette River froze and became an ice highway. His grandparents on his mother's side recalled a time when Harkins Lake was truly a lake, not like the hook-fingered channel seen on maps today. In the 1930s, the river crested, and Harkins Lake cut through close to the family house, lapping the porch steps with water. "My sister has pictures of it," says Gary. "It's just a house in the water. A lot of the houses were built up three to four steps. And back when that flood came, most of the houses had water up to two or three steps … there were a lot of stories of the army coming to rescue people, and then a lot of locals ending up rescuing the army," he says with a soft chuckle.

Even twenty-five-year-old Steve, a fourth-generation Horning, remembers the flood of 1996. He and Gary could ride in a pickup and stick their hands out the window to touch the high water. How the truck kept running, I don't know. "There was one time—he was pretty young in '96," says Gary, pointing to Steve. "But I told my wife, 'roll the windows down.' And she says, 'why?' And I said, 'if it washes us off the road we want to be able to get out.' Because you could feel the pickup moving sideways. We decided, this is just a little bit too high. We'll go back to the boat." And back to the boat they went. For a whole week, Steve took a little motorboat to school. Coming home, he used a spotlight to find his way back in the dark. The story surprises me because I remember the '96 flood. My family was inconvenienced with high water for three days, but it was nothing like the three months the Hornings had to deal with water on their land. The flood got old, both Steve and Gary admit.

I ask the Hornings how the river has changed over the years. The flood regimes are different, Gary says. More backwater areas are filling in with silt. Before all the dams and revetments, the floods were bigger, but quicker. Now the Army Corps keeps the water at bankfull longer so it lingers and doesn't clean out the sloughs. "The sloughs now are all dead," says Gary, lingering on the last word and tinting his sentence with a kind of sad resolve. "They've been dammed off at one end or the other, and they're just big stagnant ponds. You can look at the maps and tell the river has been changing forever. But we've changed the way it changes."

The Hornings are in the early stages of going through the restoration process—the planning, assessing, and long haul of permitting and monitoring. Hearing this, I want to know what restoration means to a farmer, what it means to a family with four generations of memory and stories etched in their bones. Steve says they want to open up Harkins Lake so it can provide habitat and flood storage, since it has been silting in over the years. Gary chimes in. "I'd like to see the Harkins Lake channel alive again," he says, with an almost imperceptible nod. Even when talking about a channel that has surrounded his family's farm for one hundred years, Gary is steady and economical in his movements. But his soft eyes show a wisdom and deep connection to the land and river. "It's one thing when you sit there and you grow up around it, and you slowly see channels die. We've filled a lot of channels and sloughs, even in my life ... But that one [Harkins Lake] was a real living area, and it's turning into that stagnant pond. It'd be nice for it to come back."

Ed Rust
Little Willamette, Albany

Ed Rust didn't become a farmer, even though agriculture is deep in his blood. His grandmother was a Pettibone and lived on a farm north of Corvallis where a road still bears the family name. His great uncle, Kenneth Pettibone, almost tarnished that name when he conned the family into selling the farm, took the money, and ran off with a blonde girl. He was never heard from again. Ed can flit from a poker-face deadpan to a hearty, wheezing laugh in the same sentence. Even while talking about his great uncle Kenneth and the family skeletons in the closet, he flashes a smile and then hurls a laugh straight from his chest.

The Pettibone family came to the Little Willamette property near Albany around 1920. The previous family had settled the farm through a donation land claim and built a brick house, which still stands, in the 1860s. The tall, reaching oak tree in Ed's front yard is also a relic. A descendant from the original settlers said her great grandfather was born under the tree.

Ed's father's side of the family homesteaded by Buena Vista, where one-hundred-foot sandstone walls loom over the Willamette River. There, his father raised dairy cows. He was exceptionally bright and graduated from Oregon State University at sixteen. When Ed's father and mother married, they moved to Coos Bay and continued a dairy farm operation using small but productive cows. Then McDonalds came along and small cows were of no use. The growing fast-food enterprise wanted big heifers to put into a chipper once they were done giving milk, and Ed's father couldn't compete.

Now, Ed lives on his mother's property on the Little Willamette, in the original homestead house (although an addition has since been made). Even though he didn't go into farming, he knows the Little Willamette landscape well. "If you look at the old photographs from '36, this place had a ton of wood on it," he says. Then, when the ryegrass industry got big, the wood was cleared because everyone wanted to pick up that extra acre. "In the seventies, the attitude was farm it or frame it," he said.

The other major change on Ed's land is that the Little Willamette once connected to the mainstem river and threaded across his and neighboring land. Parts of the channel have been farmed up, and it hasn't been open in "many moons," says Ed. But it does connect in some areas during high water. The winter rains come, logs pile up in the remaining channel, the water backs up, and it floods. Different environmental groups have dreams of reconnecting the Little Willamette, which will let the water move through in the spring and provide a migratory passage for fish.

Ed offers a tour of the property. I put on my mud boots and accept with a smile. With no heirs to inherit his land, Ed worked with the Greenbelt Land Trust to put a conservation easement on the property and restore it. Restoration, like farming, is in his blood. He points to a grass field where his grandfather built a wetland in the 1960s. The wetland has since returned to farmland, but Ed plans to turn it right back.

Bigleaf maple leaves crunch beneath our feet. We pass by a wetland that Ed put in a year ago, already full of geese. He's seen lesser yellowlegs, Virginia rail, northern shovelers, bald eagles, and even a golden eagle near the wetland. He plans to keep it open to benefit waterfowl. Take swans, for example. "They're like 747s," he says. "They have a long glide path and need an open area to land."

I ask how do he or the Greenbelt Land Trust know what to restore to. How do they know for sure what was here before? Rather than pretending to have an answer, he says, "Who knows what this land really was one hundred years ago? All we're really doing is putting our spin on it."

Throughout our walk he shows me parts of his land and plans for it. Part will be oak savannah with native grasses and prairie plants. Part will be open wetlands to attract waterfowl. Finally, we stop at the edge of his property and look out to his neighbor's field, where the Little Willamette used to flow and connect to the portion on Ed's land. I'm tempted to ask why not just reconnect it, but I know the reason why. The landowners don't want a channel permanently running through their field. It would chop their land in half. The channel is permanently dead, I think.

I look out at the field, mostly mud with small sprigs of green. "You can *alllllmost* see it," Ed says, his voice edged with fascination. He sweeps his hand near my face in the curve of the channel, perhaps hoping my eyes will pick up on the pattern. I humor him and say I see it, but I don't. I see a field. A dead channel.

On our walk back to his house, the wind rocks through my digital recorder. Listening to the recording later, much of it is filled with the rhythmic crunch of leaves under our boots, the whine of air moving across the land, and spells of silence. I stay much longer than I mean to, talking with Ed about nothing related to why I came. When the moment is right, I thank him for his time, and leave.

At home I pull up an aerial image of Ed's land, hoping I can see the former Little Willamette even though it's been farmed over for many years. And suddenly there it is: the shadowed mark in the land and slight depression where water once flowed. I look up and around the room, as if searching for someone to share this wondrous discovery. But I'm alone. So I keep staring at the drifting trail of the Little Willamette on my computer screen until the light outside begins to fade and evening settles in.

The Buchanans,
Tyee Wine Cellars (century farm), Corvallis

If I told the Buchanan story from start to finish with no detours, it would be no fun. It wouldn't reflect the way Dave Buchanan talks, either. Dave, an outstanding fish biologist who founded Tyee Wine Cellars with his wife, Margy, is like an anxious stream that stirs in one direction and then another, ambling around boulders before joining the main current. So I will tell the story like the spindling creek running in his mind. If coyote scat or goose honk distracts us, rest assured we will find the mainstem story at a point downstream.

The first thing I should know, Dave tells me, is that there are two creeks, or "cricks" as he says, that come together on the Buchanan farm—the Beaver and Muddy. The Beaver flows into the Muddy, which winds to the Marys, which moseys to the Willamette.

We shuffle past a grove of filberts that he and Margy planted in 1974, the year they also planted wine grapes. Neighbors thought they were crazy to be farming for wine. Some ryegrass farmers wouldn't even talk to them.

We pause to listen to the cacophony of geese wading in a sixty-three-acre wetland he recently put in. From where we stand, the geese look like a brown smudge on a watercolor painting—focused enough to catch the eye, but far away enough to dim its reality. Then a flock comes in to land. A maelstrom of geese twists in the air, spiraling down in circles tighter with each lap around. Closer to the water, they coalesce into a single moving thing, a tornado with a will of its own. Then the geese flutter and flap to break speed and kick up water when they land.

"Wow," both Dave and I say. The geese are just one kind of bird Dave sees. In total, he has identified 149 bird species on his land.

I wasn't sure how one person could tell a 125-year story in a couple hours. But I ask how the Buchanans came to settle the land anyway. His poor Scottish ancestors went gold mining in Idaho before they had enough money to buy the farm. Dave gets distracted by a 243-acre wetland restoration project he put in more than a decade ago. Flags litter the ground where they planted Nelson's checker-mallow, a native prairie forb. Dave says some trees had to be removed to keep the area open and create continuous wetlands. But he has more than made up for the trees removed. He figures he has planted more than ten thousand trees on the farm. On top of that, a thick line of riparian vegetation runs along Muddy and Beaver creeks, in some places up to six hundred feet thick. "We have about one hundred-some acres of native woods that my ancestors never touched. They were either really lazy or had an environmental ethic. Imagine pulling out huge ancient oak trees with just axes, shovels, mules, and dynamite," he says.

He goes on to explain that the first wave of settlers, who had got their land free, sold off parts of it to a second wave of settlers, such as the Buchanans. For 528 acres, his family paid $7,939 in gold coin, which was a lot of money in 1885. The high price, Dave tells me, was likely because the valley was so fertile and some areas had already been cleared by Native American burning practices.

We cut onto a small trail on his property. In the 1950s, the Soil Conservation Service wanted to straighten all the rivers and creeks to increase farmable acreage, and because they thought it would reduce flooding. They offered the service to farmers free of charge. After straightening Beaver Creek, they started on Muddy Creek. But Dave's father, an angler and hunter, thought the straightened creek looked ugly. So he stopped the program, thankfully before they carried out their plan to straighten the entire Muddy and Marys River Basin clear to the Willamette River. "I was really proud of him because that was a big thing for him to make that stand," says Dave. He guesses that if the program continued, their 3.3 miles of meandering Muddy Creek would have been reduced to a mile or a mile and a half. Today, Dave himself is a huge supporter of restoration.

We emerge from the trail and come back to an orchard of hazelnut trees. Dave stops. "What the heck are those guys?" He peers through the binoculars. "That guy flying," he points to a tall row of trees. "That's a peregrine … look at his wings, look how pointed they are. The way he flies, that's how you tell what he is. He almost flies like a pigeon." Peregrines hunt ducks on his property. They dive with speeds reaching 160 miles per hour and pounce on the duck in mid air. He's seen two separate diving kills while walking on his farm over the years.

I can't believe how much Dave knows about this land. Part of it comes from being a fish biologist for thirty years, but most of it, I suspect, comes from just living it.

Let's talk about floods, I suggest, and Dave agrees. "We flood out here a lot, partly because they straightened Beaver Creek. And now that it's straightened, it just moves the flood downstream," he says. He talks about the 1964 flood, when he was in college and courting Margy, and almost not being able to see her because of high water on the road. When he was a kid, shallow water would cut through their farm during high flows. He remembers rowing a drift boat to load up sheep in a far field and move them to higher ground. There are also rocks on his property from the Missoula Floods that crashed into the valley several thousand years ago. Nestled in icebergs and then deposited onto the valley floor, the rocks are called erratics because they don't fit the area's geologic profile.

At the end of our conversation, Dave suggests I talk to his daughter Merrilee, who is now the estate winemaker and vineyard manager. Some weeks later, I catch up with Merrilee to talk about her experiences as a young farmer growing up on a piece of land with so much family history. She has a different story to tell. As a child, she walked Beaver and Muddy creeks and caught cutthroat trout. Floods were simply a part of life. As the high waters moved in, they deposited rich alluvium onto the land, which is why there is at least one pasture the Buchanans don't have to fertilize.

But things are different now, Merrilee says. She doesn't walk or swim in the creeks anymore. They're not what they used to be. There are fewer fish. Farmers are using new and potent poisons, and the uplands are being logged, so water moves down slope at a faster rate, carrying fertilizers and other poisons to the streams. Merrilee says she cannot remember seeing so many log trucks pass by the farm. Besides the ecological changes to the land, there's not as much community among growers. She tells a story of her ancestors and surrounding neighbors all working the fields to gather hay. It doesn't happen like that now.

"Isn't it sad to see the loss of human and animal communities?" I ask.

"Yes," she says, almost cutting off my question, maybe knowing it was coming.

It's a simple answer, but that's all she needs to say. Her steady eyes fill with tears. I could have looked away, as someone might do when a stranger shares such an honest moment of emotion. But I don't look away, accepting the fragile thing being communicated between us. I catch her grief more strongly through this silence than I could have through conversation. And that's how the world would find us, if it were watching: two young women looking at each other with eyes full of tears.

Peter Kenagy
Kenagy Family Farms, Albany

The surname Kenagy—an altered spelling of Swish German *Gnaegi* or *Gnagy*—denotes someone who lives in or by his fields as opposed to in a village. Peter Kenagy honors his family name well. In his fields, which include a mile of riverfront land, he's grown native seed, a mix of vegetables, wheat, grass, and forest buffers to improve streamside vegetation. He's won awards for his innovative approach to improving soil quality, and sustainable agriculture groups have given him the nod for his early adoption of cover crops and strip tilling.

During the first part of our conversation, Peter and I sit and look out to his fields. I arrived just as the morning light splashed across the sloughs tracing his land, before the slicing cold had lifted.

His father's family acquired the first fifty acres in the early 1930s and grew pole beans, filberts, and gooseberries. Over the years, the Kenagys added to their acreage. An area with looming fir trees originally owned by a man named Sloper fell into his family's hands, and thankfully so. Sloper had dreams of turning his property into a motorcycle racetrack or even an airstrip. The piece of land with the sloughs running across it used to be owned by the Nebergall Meat Packing Company. The company changed hands a couple times, then the Kenagys acquired the land in 1985.

Peter is calm and quiet in speech but restless in his movements. He gets up from the chair to look at something, then suggests we move into his garage. Then he sits down and stands up again—to look at geese in his field, to fetch an aerial photograph of his land, or to show me pictures. I suspect this is why he has been able to manage his land so well—he has the right level of energy for a daunting task.

He shows me photos his father took of Willamette River floods. In the 1940s, his father climbed the tall fir trees on the Sloper piece of property and took a picture looking out to Spring Hill near Albany. I thought the picture was of the ocean. All I could see was water. Another photo shows a rope tied from the barn to the house. Peter explains that his father tied the rope so he could travel to the barn and milk the cows, since the current was too swift to walk across. I imagine a man holding onto a rope, crossing one hand gingerly over the other, hoping he doesn't slip into the dead-cold water.

How these floods changed his land, or all the ways the sloughs have been altered, Peter doesn't know. Looking at an aerial photograph, he surmises that the far slough running mostly parallel to the river once curved up to connect to the main channel. He also knows that one ditch on his property was blasted open with dynamite. It was dangerous work. A man died while clearing stumps on the property with dynamite.

We take a tour of his farm, and Peter details field by field how he got the land, his plan for it, and what he's growing. It's a lot of land for one person to keep track of. I keep having to re-affirm I know what he is talking about: "You mean the fifty acres your dad first acquired, right?" I would ask. Throughout his property, Peter has planted a lot of trees—firs and cottonwoods along one of his sloughs, which had been cleared for firewood by a previous owner. The slough may not look like much, but Peter says a fish biologist surveyed juvenile Chinook salmon in it. Peter would like to replace a small culvert with tidegates to allow high water to flow out unimpeded but retain continuous flow. This would improve fish habitat, Peter hopes. "Can you think of anything better than to have [Chinook salmon] restored?" he asks, still-faced and unblinking. "To have a lot of them in the Willamette again would be, I think, a crowning achievement."

Peter has also done a lot of restoration work down by the river, an area that had been heavily grazed by cattle. I sit on the back of a Honda four-wheeler as he shows me the work he's done over the years. We crisscross through black walnuts, ash, cottonwoods, through snowberry and Oregon grape. He shows me the invasives he battles too—not just blackberry and reed canary grass, but common tansy, false brome, and wild carrot. To him, invasive species are the biggest impediment to river restoration. He's also worried that agencies don't have the funds or a plan to manage all the lands acquired for restoration. "The reality is we as a society don't have the capacity to do all the restoration work that people think we need to do. We're putting the cart before the horse in some cases," he says.

By this time, I've talked with Peter for almost four hours, and it's two days before Christmas. I apologize one too many times and leave feeling like a nuisance and intruder. But the following week, Peter invites me to join two friends and him on a motorboat ride to see the Willamette's high flows. I am delighted at the chance, since I never float the river in the dead of winter with so much rain. We put in at Hyak Park near

Albany and zip up and down the brown waters of the Willamette. Entire stands of trees are underwater, and an island I had visited in the summer near Half Moon Bend is nearly submerged. Peter and his friends seem to know every curve and juncture. We pull into Frazier Slough, venture around Truax Island, stoop between willows and twigs to check the backwaters. We go down the Little Willamette and explore Bowers Rocks State Park by foot. Trudging over wet blackberries with mean thorns, I follow behind these three men. They are looking for something, but what? Somehow, I can't keep up with the names and places they are talking about. The old Berger place. The abandoned gravel pit. Horseshoe Lake.

From the thick undergrowth, a small meadow yawns open. This clearing is the place they were looking for, I find out. Somehow, the meadow has no blackberries or big fir trees on it. Somehow, it has stayed open all these years. Has it ever been farmed? If no one is managing it, why is it not overgrown with trees and invasive shrubs? Was this once a gravel bar when the river flowed through here? Could it be untouched from indigenous burning practices? Could we have found a place preserved in the amber of time?

Without reaching a conclusion about the meadow, we slog back through the underbrush and back to the boat. The three men talk about who used to own what land, and when and why certain families left. They talk about fishing and exploring old sloughs that are now filled up with silt, much like the Hornings did. It must be hard to see the places you once explored as a child disappear.

I strain to hear what they are saying, but many of their words get lost to a cold wind. I want to lean in and listen, but somehow it feels like eavesdropping on three friends. It doesn't feel right to learn the stories from a simple telling, to rob them of a thing they earned through years of watching and running the river. But a part of me wonders if some stories of a wilder Willamette will get lost like that—muffled by a cold wind, silenced by time, plugged up by silt, sealed shut by forgetting, until the stories lapse into the dim recesses of a thing long gone. I catch what I can and thank them for the boat ride.

Back home, I realize what I was looking for in these stories about the Willamette. It's the same thing Peter and his friends were looking for in the meadow—proof that such a thing exists no matter how it got there. In the same way, it doesn't matter how these stories got there, or why they remain. I'll likely never understand the route these farmers took to care about a place so much, or why they feel moved to undertake an act as selfless as restoration. Chasing that understanding would take years, far beyond the short yet valuable time I spent with them.

My search for stories of restoration wasn't about crafting a perfect map of the Willamette, both as it was and might be, but knowing that the stories of hope and resiliency existed at all and could lead me to someplace new. I was glad to hear a few tales about the place I live and about the people trying to set it right again. Under stones, in the brush, in the fields, and in the winter waters resting in a slough, the stories rose up like atoms sifting into the air.

The Grief and the Gladness

❖❖❖

I made a new friend named Erika, and I was glad for it because new friends often don't have the gumption yet to turn down an invitation—which is why Erika agreed to go kayaking when I asked her. We had met in graduate school and enjoyed sharing research ideas and advice on which classes to take and which ones to avoid.

When I made the invitation to go kayaking, I came ready with a list of assurances: It will be flat water. We will wear life jackets. Ben will show me how to use our convoluted straps again so we can load and unload the kayaks. But I didn't need any of those assurances. Erika simply said, "When are we going?"

I suggested we take a short trip to a nearby place called Colorado Lake. We could go at the end of the day but before the sun went down. A river ecologist had told me the lake was a remnant channel of the Willamette River. Stranded ponds and lakes skirt the mainstem—ghosts of the river's once-complex past. Old maps show hints of channels and sloughs that once flowed near my house, like shadowy scars. The soil under my foundation—Dayton Silt Loam, Malabon Silty Clay Loam, and Waldo Silty Clay Loam—means the plain where I live was likely a wetland before settlement. This also means developers, farmers, and landowners buried the Willamette's channels and wetlands alive by filling them with dredge sediment and building houses on top, leaving only a few scattered ponds.

When Erika and I arrived at Colorado Lake, we talked to a man with sapphire blue eyes. He told us we could use his dock, since there was no public access. We carried the kayaks down one at a time, dodging beer cans impaled on madrone tree branches and nodding to the man each time we passed.

Erika was a natural at paddling. She didn't need instruction and didn't get wet when she plopped in her kayak. On the water, she floated with ease, lifting and dipping her paddle in graceful figure eights and twisting her wrists almost imperceptibly.

Curtains of late light draped the water. We watched a yellowlegs spear bugs by the shore. Big plumes of algae topped the lake and covered our paddles when we lifted them from the water. I thought *if I were that man with sapphire blue eyes, I would be out here every day in a boat.*

Colorado Lake turned out to be pretty small and linear, so we'd float along the edge, drift for a time, and then turn around. The two of us paddled alongside damselflies with indigo bodies and white-tailed kites flapping through the air like prayer flags. We paddled and swapped stories—how Erika almost lost her husband to a mountaineering accident, the places she's lived like Chicago and Africa, and the stints she's had as an environmental activist. It was good to talk about something besides school. With light haloing her apricot hair, Erika listened as I eulogized the end of raspberry season in my parents' backyard. My stories felt small in comparison to hers.

Edward Abbey writes that people naturally have a piece of land that calls to them. For some it might be a place far away, a foreign country filled with new people and cultures. For others, it might be a stranded pond that floats two friends. As we reached the edge of the lake, an edge that once extended to the main channel, I wanted to ask Erika whether a particular soil or smell of river calls to her, bone-deep, or whether she limps heavy with the weight of a particular place. But the timing wasn't right. We didn't know each other like that. Not yet.

Even though I was flush with words and thoughts, I was completely surprised by the silence that descended upon us, like cold night air drifting across a stream. Wrapped in the silence was the weight of something unexpected—a sense of things passing or things already passed, of places that were once pristine and others that will disappear in my lifetime. My heart filled with sadness that came from thinking about this lovely, stranded river, a place both beautiful and damaged. Holding our paddles against our bodies, we were carried to a place not spoken but felt. We glided through water, unmoored and drifting, and let silence do the talking.

❖❖❖

I was browsing for books at the library when a poster caught my eye. "Grieving the Gulf—We Gather to Bear Witness," it said. Intrigued, I read further and learned that a local church was hosting a ceremony to mourn the worst environmental disaster in U.S. history: the Gulf Oil Spill. In the spring of 2010, a sea-floor wellhead blew out, killing workers and gushing oil into the Mexican Gulf. Every night on the news, pictures of dead birds with their blackened bodies and hollow stares flashed across the screen. Shrimpers were put out of business. A dark rim of oil was advancing toward the marshes. And thousands of miles away, a group was hosting an event to bear witness to the catastrophe. The gathering intended to give people a place to express their feelings about the unfolding ecological disaster and help them "move toward healing and transformation." In all my time living in Corvallis, I had never seen a funeral organized for anything but a human being, so I decided to go.

I sat in the back row of a church, among a group of people who had gathered to grieve. Sometimes in pairs, sometimes alone, the grievers filed in and prayed. They moaned, wailed, and knelt.

I went to the gathering hoping to catch grief from a nearby mourner in the same way you might catch a cold, as if grief could be felt and understood so easily. But my heart was armored with irony. The oil spill is catastrophic. It is sick, horrible, and obscene. It has killed birds, fish, shrimp, and oysters, and left communities without livelihood. Eleven people died from the oilrig blast and untold wildlife will perish from the sixty thousand barrels of oil leaking into the ocean each day. I know this. But I could not pray because I could not find the words to speak of sadness even in the privacy of my own heart. I could not sing because I doubted the reality of my voice, paranoid that someone would detect my hypocrisy. Here we were, mourning a loss caused by oil when most of us drove to the church without questioning it. And we will go home and turn on our computers and televisions and buy things shipped from places we can't pronounce. Won't this disaster take more than prayer? Is grief enough?

After a moment of silence, the church leader gave us a chance to express sorrow in our own way. People could write a poem, light a candle, put up a prayer flag, stay in their chairs, or dip their hands in water in a kind of blessing. I got up, avoiding a woman I knew, and shuffled in line to the water blessing station. I paid close attention to the men and women in front of me. They would submerge their hands for a moment, turn them over, then bring them up, sometimes touching their own forehead. When it was my turn, I tried to mimic the motions and reverence of the people before me, but I became too aware of the woman behind me, wondering if I was doing it right.

At one point, I wanted to ask a crying woman whether she grieves for the environmental disasters happening right here. Maybe, like me, she also struggled with how to mourn for something that isn't immediate like an oil spill, but something subtle and recessed. I wondered if she thought about the salmon in the Willamette Basin whose redds were dredged and spawning grounds drained; the floodplain forest, once thick along the river, now a picket fence in many places; the great blue heron rookeries that became parking lots and homes; the ninety miles of lost river channels between Eugene and Albany; the displaced and dead indigenous people who were victims of disease and cultural fragmentation. What about the fox, lamprey, larkspur, and muskrat that have perished over the years? Surely these casualties surpass the ones of the oil spill disaster. Why aren't we sad for this loss? I could have responded to my own question with a thousand answers: because forgetting is easier than confronting, because other disasters bait our attention, because the Willamette's lost channels are an invisible wound, because grieving the Willamette might be an admission of guilt, because blaming faceless oil executives is easier than blaming ourselves.

Of course I did not grab the woman by the shoulders and ask her if she grieves for the Willamette. How could I? These things do not have the shock value of an oil-slicked shorebird or decimated marsh. But who knows how many animals my house has killed or displaced, since it was built in what used to be the floodplain.

"Perhaps our grandsons, having never seen a wild river, will never miss the chance to set a canoe in singing waters," wrote Aldo Leopold. Unlike John Graves, who solemnly traveled down the Brazos before a few dams went in, and unlike Edward Abbey, who wandered through the Colorado's Glen Canyon to pay homage to its soon-to-be-gone wildness, my generation has never seen a wild Willamette, before it became a single channel. We have never had the chance to set a canoe in its singing waters and grieve for what will soon be lost. Much is already gone.

Habitat loss is like an oil spill played out in slow motion—too sluggish for us to register any real threat until it's too late. Even when we replant the trees and the land looks healed, sometimes the web of life takes decades to recover, or never will. Sometimes, we don't heal the landscape and instead keep degrading it. More than ten years ago, scientists projected what the Willamette River Basin would look like in the year 2050 under normal, conservation, and development conditions. So far, we are cruising on the development trajectory, filling more wetlands and losing more prairie habitat. This has caused and will cause cascading effects, from loss of biodiversity to altered water cycles. In many ways, our effort to control rivers increases the impact of floods.

With fewer wetlands to store water, the lag time between rain hitting the ground and entering the stream becomes shorter, which cranks up the river's power.

Standing among the oil spill grievers, I thought about the last time I had been in a church. It was more than a year before, and I'd come to honor the death of my friend's father. Limb by limb, muscle by muscle, he lost the ability to move, swallow, and breathe until he suffocated to death. When I got the call from my friend that her father had died, I wept immediately. There was no thought, only feeling. The Willamette River suffered a similar fate. Settlers disconnected the river limb by limb and cut off its circulation. Atrophied and starved of oxygen, the river in some spots could hardly support fish life. When I learned this story, I did not cry.

I tried to comfort my grieving friend by telling a Taoist story about Chuang Tzu, an ancient Chinese philosopher. When Chuang Tzu's wife died, a friend came to visit and found Chuang Tzu merrily singing. Puzzled, the friend asked how he could be so cheerful during a time of sorrow. Chuang Tzu explained that his wife was simply completing a cycle and returning back to where she came—back to a place of nonexistence. We don't grieve for people before they are born, he rationalized, so why should we grieve for them when they die? I turned to my friend, confident that my clever and profound story had uplifted her spirits. She met my smug face with tears and said, "I don't think I'm ready to be Chuang Tzu." Her reaction stung me.

Grief is a wretched yet necessary step to healing—a step toward feeling the featherweight of gladness again, and maybe the same is true for ecological loss.

When we were back in our seats, the church leader of the Grieving the Gulf ceremony invited us to make a sound to express our sadness. I let out a small whimper that I doubt even the man sitting in front of me could hear. A woman near the front let out a melodic moan that turned into a kind of song. I could not see her face, only her curly salt and pepper hair. As she began to sing, she tilted her head back and arched her song to the church ceiling. She raised her hands up one inch at a time, stopping just above her head. Her song thrummed and warbled slow and steady against the wood planks of the church. The sureness of her grief was mesmerizing. It came out strong and real. Instead of joining her, I pretended I had to go to the bathroom. I got up halfway through the ceremony, and drove home.

❖❖❖

Soon after the Grieving the Gulf ceremony, I stopped to listen to a man playing a bugle at the confluence of the Marys and Willamette rivers. I had seen this Bugle Man before, wearing his clown pants. Sometimes he walked with a dented bugle tied to his waist. It banged against his hip in rhythm with his step. Sometimes, one of these brass instruments dangled from each side. Either way, he walked with his head up high, often with a red, green, and gold Rastafarian beanie. Sometimes I'd see him by the river or in the used bookstore downtown. He was mostly alone and always walking. I don't know if he had a family or home to go to at night.

When he played, the Bugle Man would face the river. He'd blow out raw and earthy notes that stretched across wet air, thick as a dirge. His songs were streaked with the sadness only the blues can tell—sadness you might feel for a stolen sweetheart, a broken dream, an oil-filled ocean, or a strangled river. Maybe he knew he stood at Shawala Point Park, which honors the Marysville band of the Kalapuya people.

Once, I asked the Bugle Man why his songs were so sad. He just shrugged and kept playing. Another time, I stopped pedaling my bike and told him that he and the river made a nice duet. He shot me a puzzled look. The river pounded too loudly and drowned my words. I was beginning to wonder if he thought I was crazy.

This time—the time right after the Grieving the Gulf event—I did not ask the Bugle Man any questions. I sat behind a highway pillar as darkness spilled over the land. Minor notes folded into a drawn-out melody, suspended across the wrinkled lines of the Willamette. The notes from the dented bugle shuddered in a song that seemed not quite whole. The river, too, sounded in a pitch and pace different from what it used to be. Both played a dented song.

I have read that, in some aboriginal cultures, songs tell stories of the land, like audio topo maps. Each clan is a repository of songs that keep stock of the Earth's intricate grooves and bends, the swells and jagged edges. When the landscape is altered, clans still have the memory of places captured in sung storylines. I was thousands of miles away, both in distance and understanding of aboriginal culture. And yet here I was, listening to the Bugle Man's song that rang of a broken place. Songs are like testaments, keepers of knowledge, and teachers of sorrow. In music is memory, I suppose.

My hands grew cold as I listened to the bugle warbling toward a depthless sky. I hummed along, adding in a few scattered notes. Hidden behind the pillar and with the dark masking all my insecurities, I found an unexpected boldness. I hummed louder until I could feel my body softly fluttering against the concrete pillar. Intertwined in the night air, a place where a symphony of stars patters the sky and a river drums seaward, the sound of horn and song curled upward. It arched toward blackness like a whisper of grief in the dark.

❖ ❖ ❖

It's been several weeks since our community grieved the Gulf Oil Spill, and almost a year since I kayaked with Erika. The nootka roses are losing their petals, but the air is too cold for the tarweed to come out. I take a walk to the river. The water is shoving and pulling downstream, still high from a spate of last-minute rain. Around a muddy bend, water skitters like a dog running broadside into a wall after taking a corner too fast. In the hawthorns by the bank, spiders weave spokes of silk into their webs, fine strands that match the sky's clouds. From above, a great blue heron makes a distressed call and flaps dinosaur-like through the trees. His shadow trails the arc of his flight.

I walk with my head down, looking but not watching, aware, but only of the ground in front of me. The whole day I have been holding onto the most petty emotions and thoughts—the fact that I am edging toward thirty and haven't even mowed the lawn. I am feeling crummy and myopic for spending so much mental energy on one river. Maybe we should be like Chuang Tzu and just accept the death of all things. Anguishing over one river seems small, compared to the desolation in the gulf and degradation of the planet, especially when I did not witness the Willamette's original wounding.

Between breaths I step from shadow into sunlight and finally look up. The whole world crouches in a stillness I haven't felt in a while. Yet there is so much movement—birds flitting, branches quaking. So much life. Even the deep hush comes with birdsong—the nasal cry of nuthatches, the creaking-door call of the towhee, the *wichity-wichity* of the common yellowthroat. The birds sing even when there are many reasons not to.

A river has a way of blunting worry in the same way it tumbles a jagged stone. If I had not stopped in this patch of sunlight and slowed to listen to this silence and song, I might have forgotten that the world can be many things—stillness and movement, quiet and sound, even grief and gladness. I might have forgotten that these things come unexpectedly and without intention, which is what makes them real.

Bearing witness to the Willamette's long-gone wounds might mean learning to pay attention. Pay attention, and you feel. You begin to hear the land and learn its scars. Pay attention, and things beneath you become visible. In attentiveness we find unexpected silence to honor things lost, a song that holds the memory of the land, a patch of sunlight among shadowed forms.

I don't know whether we express sorrow best in silence with a friend, among strangers in a church, or in the dark listening to a broken song. But with friends there is also laughter, in church there is also rejoicing, and in the dark there is also starlight. There is always another side. Often the making of our life gets stuck under the shoulder of a stone, or spills into a dark pool. But even these deep places feel the splash of sun dappling the surface. Even jagged stones washed by current have a smooth side.

So I smile. Big. And my heart thumps happy.

I stand in the sunlight for a long time before picking up a stone near the river's shore. One side is smooth and river kissed, the other rough. I hold the stone in my hand for a while, feeling the simultaneous soft and hard of it, and then throw it in the river.

Trees, Weeds, and Rivers:
The Work of Restoration

"Ecological restoration is a practice of hope; hope because restorationists
envision a better future as a result of their efforts. Ecological restoration
is a practice of faith; faith because restorationists work in a world of
uncertainty. Finally, ecological restoration is a practice of love; love because
restorationists care about, and give their lives to, efforts that protect and
enhance the lives of humans and other-than-human beings alike."
—From *Human Dimensions of Ecological Restoration*

Trees

The rain came as soon as I arrived to plant trees by the Willamette River.
Everywhere I looked, other volunteers shrugged into jackets and shuffled
to stay warm. I fumbled with my gloves, put them on, then took them
off to see what felt best. It's hard to grab a sapling and plant it with thick
gloves. It's also hard to do it when the winter cold goes sub-surface and
numbs your hands. I decided to go with gloves.

To plant a tree, you have to decide what belongs where. If it's a cottonwood that needs the water table to grow, you plant it by the river. If it's a Willamette Valley ponderosa pine—once abundant in the area—you plant it farther upland, although I have seen a variety that likes to get its feet wet. The best time to plant a tree is when the seedling is dormant, which, in the Willamette Valley, means during a time of likely rain and definite cold. Which is also why all of us volunteers were out here in wintertime, holding construction-orange buckets stuffed with saplings.

A volunteer coordinator corralled us to demonstrate how to plant a tree. He had that Forest Service look—evergreen jacket, black boots, tan hat with the bill in a perfect curve and official-looking logo stitched on the front. He told us that the holes had been pre-dug, but we'd have to deepen them since they had filled in with mud because of the rain. He shoveled out mud with the speed and dexterity of a pro, plunging in the blade, bringing up mud, dumping it with a slight turn of the wrists, all in a continuous motion. Then he grabbed a sapling, placed it in the hole, and kicked in dirt with a deft sweep of his boot.

To plant a tree, you have to dig deep and wide enough to hold the sapling's roots. You have to make sure the top root is covered with a healthy layer of soil. Then, you have to fill the hole back in and tamp it down with your boot or the backside of your shovel.

Today we would plant rows and rows and rows of cottonwood, ash, and Willamette Valley ponderosa pine to build up the Willamette's riparian zone and convert this pasture back to a functioning floodplain. The volunteer coordinator explained that restoration is part of his group's conservation strategy. First and most importantly, they preserve intact land before it becomes too degraded, then they work to improve its ecological function. We cannot perfectly replicate the vanishing prairies of the Willamette Valley if we don't know what those conditions are, he said. In short, we need the wild. With nature's perfect template in hand, we can plant trees with a better understanding of how to provide homes for wildlife and food for the river, as well as prevent runoff from pouring into the river too fast and causing erosion.

I paired up with a thin, grinning girl with perfect olive skin, maybe in her mid-twenties. Her fine brown hair, bejeweled with silver raindrops, wisped around her narrow face. We took turns shoveling and placing a tree in the ground. The gloves were already working against me. The sapling roots tangled and twisted so when I grabbed one from the bucket, all the others came with it. Off with the gloves.

At first, each tree took us a minute or so to plant. We fumbled with the shovel while trying to find the exact hand position to maximize leverage. With my arms already weighted by the inertia of cold and rain, the shovel felt bulky and leaden. The grain of the wood pressed against my hand, at times grating it. Some holes were narrow, which meant we lost our leverage because we had to dig with the shovel nearly vertical. This also meant we had to dig tiny scoops at a time, not like the deep, deft digs that the volunteer coordinator had shown us. Even with my gloves off, I had to untangle sapling roots from the bucket. With rigid kicks, we pushed the mud back into the hole, picking up a thick ring of brown sludge on the inside of our boots. Tamping down the hole was even worse. More of the mud stuck to our boots than stayed on the ground. Sometimes, our sapling was crooked (most of the time my fault), so we had to pull it out and start again. Then, after a few rounds of the same old thing (dig, drop, fill, tamp, repeat) we cut our time in half.

We finished one long bending row and started another, stuffing the cottonwoods, ash, and pines into pre-dug holes, until we ran out of saplings. I slogged one boot in front of the other toward the buckets still full of trees, loath to start again, wasting whatever time I could by talking to strangers: "Boy, we're making progress, aren't we?" "You having fun in this rain?" Whatever it took to make this day go faster.

My partner and I started on a third row and talked about our experience with restoration. This was her first time doing a tree plant, she said, smiling. I didn't ask, but I wondered what she thought about this kind of work, whether her smile indicated happiness to be toiling in the rain on a Saturday morning or hid a deep resentment.

To plant a tree, you have to face the simultaneous sweat from labor and arthritic cold, the misery of toil, and the winter rain seeping into your bones. With planting comes mud caked everywhere, the suctioning sound of your bootsteps, and an ache in your back from stooping over and over. Then, there's the intense desire to wipe your face with a glove or hand that's already too dirty. The worst is perhaps the sour stench coming from inside your jacket. I am usually careful not to lift my arms too high while working so I don't offend anyone.

Despite the wetness and cold, I soon fought overheating. Laboring under three layers will do that. I removed my hat, and sweat clumped hair across my forehead so it looked like a comb over, or at least I imagined it that way. I looked around, and people were mostly stooped and focused on the task, the robotic stuffing of trees. Dig, drop, fill, tamp, repeat. Dig, drop, fill, tamp, repeat. It all seemed so mechanical. What were we doing out here anyway, in the wet-ripe cold when we could be at home under a blanket?

This is what environmental philosopher Andrew Light asks when he questions whether restoration can help people build a relationship with nature. His answer? That working to remedy a past ecological harm ties us to the land in important ways.

I had no doubt that restoration could build a positive relationship with nature, and that it should, but I wasn't sure if the work I was doing could get me there. Was I missing something? Could a single episode of planting tree after tree in pre-dug holes form a valuable connection to the land? What Light doesn't mention is that, even if the work is benevolent, it's damn hard. All of us volunteers were workhorses, laborers for the cause, mass muscles for the task at hand. Plus, relationships take time. They also need context to help people understand the combination of circumstances and events that shape a person or place. This is why we like to know where people have been in their lives, to understand where they are going and how we might fit in with their future travels. It might be the same for the bottomlands we were trying to replant. I hoped that we would come back to care for the trees and watch them grow so we could feel invested in the success of the project, or that we could learn more about what this place used to look like throughout the last several decades, and what the people in charge hoped it might become. Some framework might give purpose to our actions.

But maybe nothing was missing from this experience. If only I could have changed my attitude and forgotten about the immediacy of my whimpering muscles and focused on the long-term good we were trying to do.

Somehow, my tree-planting partner and I finished another row and started filling in random holes. "We're doing so good!" she exclaimed. It was the only words we had spoken besides an interjecting grunt or sniff in at least twenty holes. We were close to the river but had run out of cottonwoods and ash. All that were left were the ponderosa pines that needed to be planted further upland. The small climb to get there seemed impossible. My belly rumbled. The backs of my legs were damp from the rain creeping up and through my pants.

"Can we plant the ponderosa pines this close to the water?" I asked a volunteer coordinator, my brow knitted and voice reduced to the pitch of a begging seven-year-old.

"Sure why not," he replied. Pity works. It was close to quitting time. We had planted lots and lots of trees. A few ponderosas down by the river wasn't the end of the world.

To plant a tree, or many trees in this case, you have to fight that urge to slow down and quit, that schoolyard temptation to slack off while the teacher isn't looking. You also have to fight the growl in your muscles, the well-known signal that your body needs food, sleep, or both.

With our buckets emptied, the volunteers re-grouped to finish the even less glamorous part of the work of restoration. To plant a tree, you don't just plant trees. You clean boots and buckets, sort shovels and gloves. You load and haul things up into work trucks and vans. By the end of the day, your back and arms are tight from bending over and shoveling. And if you don't switch arms while shoveling or loading, one side of your body will be screaming at you.

As it happened, I plowed through the urge to quit and the plaguing tired eyes. The shovels were loaded, the dirty boots and gloves put away. Volunteers slowly disappeared into vans and trucks after drying up, with little energy for kinship or long goodbyes. My thin grinning partner and I took the same van back to where we had parked our own cars or bikes. She said she was tired but kept smiling anyway. Either she was a good liar or had a lot more stamina than I could muster. I turned toward the window to avoid conversation. Instead of feeling close to this place, the way Andrew Light suggests is possible by working closely with the land, all I felt was the faint tremor of muscles and that wonderful sensation of sitting down after a time of exertion. So that day, with mud-battered boots and an ache from wet and hard work, I gathered my things, and I went home.

Weeds

To pull a weed ... now that requires a whole different mindset than tree planting. It requires an adversarial sense of what *doesn't* belong, an almost violent tirade against living things we're told to hate: Scotch broom, tansy, Japanese knotweed, teasel, Himalayan blackberry, Queen Anne's lace, knapweed, bull thistle, false brome, and more. Weeds with thumb-thick roots that don't want to come up. Weeds with seeds that can lay dormant for years. Weeds that crowd out native vegetation and homogenize streamsides. Weeds with stinky residues when you pull them. Weeds with dagger thorns. Weeds that insist upon being weeds, the unwanted of our landscapes.

One morning in May, I volunteered with a small group of mostly baby boomers and students to remove Himalayan blackberry at Dixon Creek, an urban stream that flows into the Willamette. This variety of blackberry can evoke ambivalence in western Oregonians. It perfumes the air with sweet berries in August, drawing pickers who want to make jam and pies. Often you see children emerge from bushes of blackberries with syrupy smiles and purple-stained fingers. But Himalayan blackberries hedge miles and miles of highways, streamsides, and other disturbed ground. They take over yards and fields, spreading by the tips of their canes and by seed. In fact, Himalayan blackberry is one of the most costly weeds to manage in western Oregon.

98

I had no feelings of ambivalence with my loppers, shovel, and grub hoe, armed at the ready for manual-powered shrub killing. This was not like planting a tree in the bitter rain. This was lopping, digging, and whacking before the spring sun arced over the alders and beamed down our backs. This was covering our skin to avoid getting pricked but accepting the sweat streaking down our underarms. The blackberries would cling to our clothes, releasing themselves only as we yanked free.

We got started almost right away, with just a brief talk on blackberries. Most of us, young and old—the grey haired and graduate students alike—had dug blackberries before, even in our own yards. To remove a blackberry weed, you have to lop off the canes and take away the threat of thorns before you can begin digging. Then, you dig down and find what I call the brain, the blackberry's knotty center with fibrous roots emerging from it. To kill the weed, you have to find the brain, unless you have a mega mower and a huge bucket of chemicals.

Without saying much (just occasional yelps of pain from the thorns), and with cold stares, I beheaded canes. *Lop lop lop.* I mostly kept to myself and worked alone. I dove into the maw of blackberries, a tangled mess of thick green canes. When I had lopped several of them, I'd pull them out from the thicket and throw them in a pile to be hauled away. Even when severed at the base, the blackberry canes looked alive and mean with thorns. Some canes had a clean cut when I lopped them straight off. But if I got the angle wrong and had to twist and pull with the loppers, woody tassels dangled from the ends. With enough lopping, our piles of beheaded blackberries swelled to a small mountain. Our kill count grew. I smiled.

The work, no matter how satisfying, gives me pause. Blackberries are not all bad. They provide habitat for birds, stabilize the bank, and filter sediments from streamside water. Besides, to pull a weed means killing something. I was killing a thing (and enjoying it!!) so that something else could live. I had decided in my mind what didn't belong and what deserved to die. Somewhere, in the making of my morals, in all my genes and experiences, and in all the elements that had come together to make who I was, I had decided it was okay to destroy blackberries.

And even if it's okay to pull a weed, should we also kill invasives with consciousness, such as nutria and starlings?

Weeds are just part of the picture. Scores of pond fish, for example, were brought over to the Pacific Northwest, often to remind settlers of the land they had left. Why fish salmon and steelhead when you could fish the familiar carp and bass of your home waters? Some fish were intentionally planted in Oregon streams—even by esteemed entities such as the United States Fish Commission—while others made great escapes from holding ponds as rivers crested. In the late 1800s, Captain John Harlow's juvenile carp in Troutdale made a leap for it when the Columbia's backwater flooded his nursery ponds. The implications of our early fish implantations linger. Of the roughly sixty fish species in the Willamette River Basin today, half are invasive.

What to do about such unintentional folly? Do we eradicate nutria, bullfrogs, bass, blackberry, purple loosestrife, house sparrows, and all manner of other don't-belongs from our landscapes, even when they could come back? Or do we kill enough to keep them in check? What amount of death and destruction do we allow for the sake of restoration? When I ask myself these questions, restoration becomes about something more than science, or what's good for species diversity and richness, but about human values.

Restoration requires people to place worth on certain species, functions, and aesthetics. Native trees belong. Invasive blackberries do not. But placing a higher value on certain living things brings up another set of puzzling questions. If the landscape is always in flux, with things coming and going, then why do we insist on putting a top prize on native species? What is native anyway? How long does something have to be around for it to be considered "from here"? Plants disperse by wind and animal, but for some reason people hate the ones dispersed by their own means. These have been common concerns for wildlife biologists and managers, restorationists, and philosophers alike, though I suspect less common for everyday people like me.

❖❖❖

Once we had hacked down a patch of Himalayan blackberries, we got to digging. I loved when I'd pull a long root runner that would lead me straight to the brain. I made adroit, deft strokes with the grub hoe, then tried to uproot the thing with a shovel. But the blackberry was firmly wedged in the sun-dried dirt. I whacked some more. Expletives pinged across my brain, and there it was, that primal emotion called rage.

Mary Oliver writes in her poem, "For Example," that fury sometimes helps us to not feel overpowered: "some things have to feel anger, so as not / to be defeated / I love this world, even it its hard places." I'm not sure I felt love, but I did feel anger that exasperated and inspired. *I cannot be defeated. I will not be defeated.* I hacked and dug, muscles flexed and jaw clamped tight, striking and shoveling in rhythmic strokes. I forgot about everyone around me and may have even been twisting my face in disgust. *Whack! Whack! Whack!* Finally, I uprooted the brain with severed shoots sprouting from it and lifted the dreaded thing above my head in triumph. If anyone were watching, I might have looked like Perseus holding the severed head of Medusa. *I win, you bullying blackberry.* Then, I looked over, and thickets of the beast ran the length of the stream—feet and feet and feet of it.

To pull a weed, you have to focus on the small wins. Otherwise, you will just get frustrated. You have to match the weed's tenacity with your own. But this is hard to do.

A fellow volunteer stopped her digging and lopping. Like me she was a graduate student at Oregon State. With wavy auburn hair pulled back from her face, she wiped her forehead with the back of a gloved hand. In a breathy voice she exclaimed: "What kind of idiot brought these here in the first place?"

Indeed.

Rivers

People are talking about reconnecting rivers—removing man-made barriers, deepening former channels so they flow again, and re-routing stranded ponds to become part of the river. But I have no stories of this kind of restoration work yet. I have never toiled shoulder to shoulder with someone to connect a stream and have no idea what it's like. I cannot tell you whether channel reconnection is about what belongs and what doesn't, whether it's methodical work or full of malice. It could be all or none of those things.

But I imagine reconnecting a river is more sophisticated than anything I've done. Beyond toil, there is modeling, data collection, and engineering. People simulate flows and calculate gradients. They look at historical maps and flood regimes, comparing them to current data and maps generated from remote sensing. They model and map in hopes that these off-channel habitats will allow aquatic creatures to hide from predators, find shelter from swift current, and rest in the cooler water during the warm months.

I've been reading and hearing more about rebuilding channels. The Freshwater Trust, a local environmental group, put in a series of five alcoves at Woods Creek, a stream west of Corvallis in nearby Philomath. The Little Willamette, the channel I traveled down with Peter Kenagy and his friends, is one potential area that environmental groups would like to reconnect to the mainstem. In another project, Willamette Riverkeeper and other groups have been trying to reconnect nearly two miles of remnant channel and oxbow lake to the river at Willamette Mission State Park. For now, the project has been halted because of opposition from neighbors, but if the plan were to go forward, the Riverkeeper would remove three human-made barriers and sediment from the remnant channel to open it up. They would use bobcats and tractors to scrape and dig. The earthmovers that built roads and changed our landscapes are now being used to put the earth back.

Even though I don't know how to reconnect a river, there is a terrible dilemma at work here. The bulldozers puncture and scrape the land. They kill, rip, and destroy, sometimes indiscriminately. They could scoop out earth to reconnect a stream, and maybe the water will fill the new channel, but if the river decides to flow somewhere else, fish and other aquatic animals could become stranded and die. If the bulldozers can't get around the trees, maybe they rip them out. There can be an awful amount of destruction for restoration.

A farmer once gave me a tour of a thirty-acre restoration site where he and a friend had mowed all the blackberries, reed canary grass, and common tansy to prepare for re-seeding with native plants. I commented how often we destroy things in the name of restoration. Without skipping a beat, the farmer nodded firmly, saying that restoration is like remodeling a house. You knock down a wall. You make a mess. You go backwards before going forwards.

At least someone was being honest about the work.

❖❖❖

More than one hundred years ago, George Perkins Marsh urged people to replant the forests. In 1878, Frederick Law Olmsted concocted a plan to sow native plants in a Boston salt marsh that had been degraded by raw sewage. And landscape architect Jens Jensen envisioned returning the landscapes of Chicago parks to pre-European conditions. People have been talking about the meaning of restoration since it became a formal profession in the 1980s and probably before that.

Given its deep-rooted history and many forms—planting trees, pulling weeds, reconnecting rivers—what *is* restoration?

I've thought about this question a lot: while riding my bike down a path next to the Willamette, while showering in water from the same river, while mowing the lawn, while toiling with restoration volunteers, and admittedly while in conversation with close friends. So I made a list of a few ways I've thought about restoration, which have been common threads within the restoration dialogue:

Instead of definition, should we use metaphor to understand restoration? When I find myself chasing my own tail in pursuit of meaning and definition, when science and engineering alone do not bring me to truth, I turn to metaphor. One profound metaphor about the strenuous yet attuned work of restoration is that it is a "re-storying" of nature. "Re-storying the landscape will allow the roots of ecological restoration to grow deep within our consciousness," writes Gary Nabhan. "To truly restore these landscapes, we must also begin ... to make them the lessons of our legends, festivals and seasonal rites." We re-story landscapes with the norms, values, worldviews, and biases most dear and understandable to us. The values that inspire and give meaning to restoration become reflected in the outcome of our great work—to ensure future ecological certainty. What story are we scrawling on our landscapes right now as we preserve and bring resiliency to the land? And what might be my small contribution to that tale?

Is restoration about going back in time? Pretending for a moment that planting trees, pulling weeds, and reconnecting rivers all constitute restoration, then we need to consider what we are trying to restore to: pre-European settlement? Pre-destruction? Pre-human?

An acquaintance of mine once suggested the word *restoration* is a misnomer because the thing being restored will never be what it was, meaning we can't go back in time. When you darn a sock, the sock may have the same function and appearance as before, but it is *not* the same sock. For this reason, he never uses the word *restoration*, but *repair*. If repair is a better word, then when I plant trees, I am not really returning to a pre-European settler landscape. And when I remove blackberries, I am not going back to before that damn weed was brought to the Willamette Valley. I'm repairing the land to return similar function, but the land itself is not what it was.

Is restoration about bringing function back to a landscape? If this is true, then my tree planting is for habitat, erosion control, flood storage, and a nutrient source for the stream. My vicious weed pulling is to create complex habitats that favor threatened species. Reconnecting channels restores floodplain function and creates refuge areas. Restoration is then not an ideal pursuit of past landscapes, but a practical attempt to repair natural processes.

Should restoration involve people? Practically speaking, involving people is key—scientists and citizens alike. You only have to look at projects like the Little Willamette to understand why: the project was halted because of local opposition. Then there's the famous Chicago Forest Preserve District, where in the mid-'90s, citizens became outraged at a poorly publicized restoration plan that involved cutting trees and introducing prescribed fire.

I've seen the good work of common citizens—my thin grinning partner, students, and retirees—and I've grunted next to people with incredible will and unspoken drive to help a former pasture or urban creek. Even sophisticated projects, such as channel reconnections, might benefit from our contributions, however basic. Yet I wonder how to take restoration beyond a judgment of what species belong, and toward an exploration of where landscapes belong in our lives, and indeed where we belong in them.

Philosophically speaking, involving people is complex, even controversial. If restoration means creating a place free of human disturbance, then we must consider whether it's right to intervene in the name of restoration. If, on the other hand, we restore with an understanding that humans are also part of the landscape, then perhaps we don't need to restore at all since even our destructive actions could be considered natural. All my toil in planting trees and pulling weeds would be unnecessary. Of course this last argument is ultimately destructive.

Does restoration make destruction more permissible? If a group of volunteers can replant the Willamette River bottomlands, what's to stop us from destroying them in the first place? Does restoration give us the false sense that we can put it all back?

Is it better to pre-store? Maybe restoration, repair, or rehabilitation is too dependent on past scenarios or maps anchored in times long gone. Should we exact the conditions likely to occur in the future, rather than in the past? This might be a good idea, considering the unprecedented effects of climate change, increased populations, and new and nefarious pollutants. There is no map or history book that can prepare us for that. One day I could do a tree planting with saplings better adjusted to a warmer climate. Maybe pre-storation, in these times, is a wiser course, but maybe it isn't. Tinkering with nature and thinking we understand how it will respond are what got us into this mess to begin with.

❖❖❖

Of course there are many other ways to think about restoration, but I wonder if we should be questioning the *why* of it. And really, the why of restoration might be an extension of what it is. Maybe we can make progress on what it means if we understand its purpose.

So why do I go out in the rain and heat, alongside strangers and people I may never see again? I have a few theories:

I restore out of personal guilt. As I have mentioned, my home is in the floodplain, and I know that my house has buried wetlands and channels. In reality it shouldn't be there, and perhaps hundreds of trees were cleared for my neighborhood. In some way I feel obligated to right a wrong and replant the trees that were cut down for my comfortable living. I did not wield the ax. I did not fill the wetlands and sloughs, or light the fuse to dynamite the stumps. But I am benefiting from those destructive actions by living in the one-hundred-year floodplain, which really would be the ten-year floodplain had we not regulated the river so much.

I restore to feel good about it. Even if it's the perfunctory, repetitive actions of tree planting, or the aggressive nature of pulling weeds, paying my dues will give rise to a smug satisfaction of having done my work for the world.

I restore out of an honest love of the land. I hope the reason behind my small attempts at restoration is beyond ego, guilt, or a quid pro quo exchange. I'm hoping that these experiences and others like them will build a relationship with the land, the kind that Andrew Light talks about. Writers, thinkers, and environmentalists have explored the topic too. Writer Stephanie Mills says that restoration should be the transformation of our souls. We work with the land to restore a feeling of "awe in something besides our own conceits." Scholar Gretel Van Wieren writes that, in restoring the land, we too, are in important ways restored to land.

Nearly seventy years ago, Aldo Leopold wrote a profound book that reflected on the human-land relationship, perhaps as deeply as any other environmental text. He writes that the virtues and respect of the "man-man society" should be indistinguishable from the man-land society.

106

That is, our community ethic should not only include people, but place: "In short, a land ethic changes the role of *Homo sapiens* from conqueror of the land-community to plain member and citizen of it." Leopold reflects on the quality of our actions and state of mind, concluding that we need love and humility in our *perceptions* and *interactions* with the land.

Even the wisest of environmental writers tells me it's possible to restore an ethic of concern for the land. What this relationship looks like, and how and when it comes isn't always clear. But I keep trying to help the Willamette River. I pull, hack, plant, shovel, and tamp. It's doggedly hard and sometimes discouraging, and it may not reflect the purest of intentions. Yet, in whatever way I engage with the land, I search to feel the work of restoration in the ache of my hands and the ringing of my heart.

The Daily Braid

❖ ❖ ❖

9/20/2010

Against a gray sky, the only obvious color is the screaming orange of our life jackets. Stray paddles and straps litter the dew-washed ground, and four deflated rafts sit like wrinkled skins waiting to be pumped up. A dank cellar scent clings to the air, a smell all of us will come to know deeply in the next four days. We are students from Oregon State University and the University of Oregon. Some are barely old enough to legally drink. Others are entering second careers. Some are self-described fish squeezers and river rats, while a few have never gripped a paddle. We gather under this gloomy damp sky to learn about restoration on the Willamette River. When I signed up for the joint OSU-U of O course, called *Introduction to River Restoration and Planning*, I wanted to understand what restoration meant to policymakers, farmers, scientists, and thinkers young and old, and how to weave together their different ideas. But I had no idea of everything we would explore during this four-day raft trip along the Willamette's mainstem.

I know a couple people on the trip—one, a friend whom I've been fortunate to have class with every term since she started her program in water policy a year ago. The other I met during a different field course. Otherwise, these people are strangers to me.

Our launch point is Armitage Park, just north of Eugene. The U of O Ducks and OSU Beavers keep to their own kind, and we pack our sleeping bags, tents, dry sacks, and day bags in rafts with heads lowered and the same awkwardness of a first date. Better to avoid eye contact than get caught in an accidental conversation with a stranger. Somehow, through nonverbal cues, we divvy up tasks. The students who look like former river guides, the ones who brought their own life vests and wear hats with fly-fishing logos, inflate rafts and strap in metal frames with ease and dexterity. Others move coolers from one place to another in order to appear busy. The naïve enthusiasts, such as myself, try to help with tasks outside their knowledge. Right now I am trying to unweave a strap that someone has looped into a beautiful, intricate knot. Then, a fisheries and wildlife student shows me how to undo it by simply tugging on the end. "Oh. Thanks," I say, keeping my head down.

But I have to give him my attention, because he's showing me how to weave such a knot. "You make a loop, and then a loop ..." he says, curling the strap upon itself in rhythmic sweeps.

"Ohhhhhh, okay," I say, feigning comprehension. "I think I can do that." I lie.

Soon we gather in a circle, standing far enough apart to not touch elbows. It's always the same: name, program, and something about yourself—this time, something we like. Most of the University of Oregon students are in the landscape architecture program, and many like gardening. The OSU students come from engineering, water policy, water science, environmental science, and fisheries and wildlife, among other disciplines. Somewhere between a blonde-haired girl and a guy with glasses, I stop listening and think about what I will say. It's my turn and I say the last banal thing my brain lands on: My name is Abby Metzger. I'm in the environmental sciences master's program at OSU. I like writing and fantasizing about what my life will be like after graduate school. The last part spurs some courtesy laughs.

After a brief talk on river safety, we hit the churning green waters of the McKenzie River, a major tributary of the Willamette. Four rafts caravan with the current, strung together by an imaginary leash and zigging along the axis of highest velocity called the thalweg.

I am fortunate to have guest speaker Joe Moll of the McKenzie River Trust (MRT) and Stan Gregory, a fisheries and wildlife professor at OSU, in my boat. The two volley information about the Willamette River Basin, and we all listen intently. I learn that 40 percent of the water flowing under the bridges in Portland comes from the McKenzie River, a fact that, despite our tendency to compartmentalize the natural world, confirms the linkages between waterways. Most of us think of the main channel when we think of the Willamette, but, as I am beginning to realize in the short time I've been in this raft, it's also the groundwater, the rain, the upland habitats, the tributaries, the mists rising over the coastal hills, the clouds sliding down the ridge of the Cascades. Reaches are not segmented and tributaries do not behave as independent limbs. Eugene flushes and Corvallis opens up the tap, Stan says, which is a more scatological way of saying we all live downstream.

In places the river kicks and swoops around fallen trees, and we have to dig our paddles in to avoid going down a wrong channel or slamming into riprap. Initially, we are out of sync, slapping each other's paddles or inadvertently splashing one another. On top of that, my life jacket, which keeps riding up despite being cinched tightly, makes me feel like a turtle slinking its neck into the safety of its shell.

Stan politely gives us commands: *all forward, left forward right back,* or *dig dig dig*. With enough practice, we paddle through water stippled by white-capped riffles, all of us heaving together in rhythmic strokes. Another group isn't as lucky and loses a passenger off the side of the raft. Since our boat is the leader, we don't see it happen, but apparently two students hauled him back in, and not a moment after, he was smiling though sopping wet. Nothing like a little danger to break the ice.

A few times we have to get out and portage through shallow water, but it helps that we have Randy, an OSU Fisheries and Wildlife researcher, as our scout and equipment schlepper. Several times, he glides ahead in his motorboat, saddled with thirty-some backpacks, and reports back on the channel conditions so we know what to avoid.

Joe points to landmarks along the way. One is a tall cottonwood gallery forest growing inland—a former channel of the McKenzie, Joe tells us, his blue eyes peering from under the curved rim of his hat. The floods came, rearranged the river's course, and spun it in new direction.

The drone of gravel-mining operations pollutes the soundscape as we paddle by Confluence Island—named for the confluence of the Willamette and McKenzie rivers. To feel the difference in temperature, Joe has us stick our hands in the McKenzie and then Willamette as it flows in. The Willamette is warmer—in places too warm to support native fish. Sight may be our strongest sense, but touch can tell a truth our vision hides. Feel the river. Touch it. Smell it. That's how you'll come to learn what it is.

❖❖❖

A few miles downstream from our launch point, all four rafts pull over on a gravel bar adjacent to a backwater area where a small native fish called the Oregon chub has recently been found. Stan tells us chub were once common up and down the river. But since they require slow-moving, complex, and heavily vegetated areas, chub have been reduced to isolated pockets. If we want to restore the land to increase fish populations, we would have to re-create these complex habitats. That might mean planting trees, reconnecting channels, or creating alcoves and sloughs with backhoes, not to mention a lot of modeling and engineering. Landowners next to a channel reconnection project might resist. The re-channeled water could flood their property, cut into their land, or reduce their acreage and income. Restoration, even when coming from a place of good intention, can have unforeseen consequences.

As Stan tells us this, I see everyone's faces growing more perplexed. Some stare or furrow their brows. As students in environmental and ecological programs, we're told restoration is always a good thing, but suddenly the picture is growing more complex. There are more strands in this knot than the environment.

There are many things about the river and restoration that I have yet to learn. But right now, I am standing in a circle with other students, on a gravel bar, next to the Willamette, wondering how to restore this huge, powerful river. And people are framing restoration in new ways. Joe says we shouldn't restore to meet the minimum requirements of ecosystem function, of beauty, of habitat, or whatever other aspect we're trying to restore. We should restore for wealth. Why shouldn't we go beyond marginal solutions and try to repair nature's riches? This is why we have imagination of course, to plunge the deep reaches of possibility.

After a good twenty minutes of discussion, we offer our silence to the river. I hear the drone of sand and gravel machines, the furtive chirp of song sparrows. I smell the trailing scent of pine and sweat, and finally I feel a deep swell of something in my chest. I am glad to be among these strangers floating downstream.

❖❖❖

We are getting hungry and stop at Green Island, a parcel of land being restored by the MRT. A light breeze waves through the grass. We sit and eat our lunches on an open swath of land in a circle that seems tighter than our launch point a few hours ago. Here, countless people have planted more than fifty thousand native trees and shrubs, re-converting more than two hundred acres of agricultural field back to floodplain forest. In addition, they are improving seasonal links to sloughs and river alcoves. A huge levee once disconnected the river from the floodplain, but MRT workers removed three Olympic-sized pools of sediment and material to let the river back in.

It might seem counterintuitive to let a river spill onto adjacent land— why would we ever value a flood? For one thing, Joe and others from

MRT explain, connecting a river to its floodplain flushes out sediment and refreshes spawning areas for fish. Side channels also provide natural areas for the river to store and dissipate its floodwaters. Once the water recedes, nutrients from the land enter into the stream system and benefit aquatic animals.

I ask Joe if what they are trying to do here is go back in time, as if nature were a series of frozen images that we can replicate. No, he says, confirming my own belief and what others have said. You can't really go back, just get the clock ticking again. The goal is to restore function and process, in this case by allowing the river access to its floodplain.

I think about how the MRT may not realize the full return of their laborious investment for decades. Think about the thousands of trees they planted. They won't be full grown until the person who planted them is likely gone and passed. The thought reminds me of when I planted trees with middle school students on land near the Little Willamette. As we were cleaning up, one student lingered behind, and I assumed she was goofing off. I went to get her, and saw her crouching around a cottonwood sapling, carefully patting the dirt until the tree was absolutely straight. So much care for a tree that might outlive her. So much care for a tree she might never climb or see fully grown.

It's strange that we pay this kind of sweat equity toward the future promise of ecological healing. Some environmental philosophers, like Eric Katz, have argued that we do this out of arrogance, thinking we know nature well enough to rebuild it. Under the guise of helping the land, we are really helping ourselves and repairing landscapes to reflect human values. But I think these philosophers are framing their argument in the same human-centered worldview they are criticizing. They are thinking of restoration in human timescales. The act itself *is* marred with human design and intervention. But there likely won't be evidence of our forgery in five hundred years, a thousand years, or ten thousand years. Imagine Green Island overgrown with tall, stooping trees and a thick understory of snowberry and deer ferns. Imagine it

114

with quiet pools and alcoves with a western pond turtle stretching its neck to greet the morning sun.

Restoration is not a single act at all, but part of a continuum of healing that carries on long after we are dead. We plant a gallery forest in the knowledge that we will never run through it, but that a river may. This requires a humble awareness of our connection to and dependence on the earth. This means caring for the land and its future inhabitants. There has to be room for wonder and love of landscapes, the sense of something larger than ourselves. If not, what will stop us students from getting out of these rafts and not caring? Just pull the string and the knot comes undone.

❖❖❖

The first night we camp on Blue Ruin Island. My one friend and I survey the spot. We brought tents but decide to sleep out in the open, even though we know the dew will slick our sleeping bags. We know this because two weeks ago, we slept without tents on a different island on the Willamette and woke up with dew on our eyelashes.

Randy, our scout and equipment manager, shows us what he calls a beaver superhighway—a long narrow path with dozens of prints and flattened areas from where beaver have dragged sticks and tails. My friend and I smile at each other. We find a small plateau adjacent to the superhighway and stake our sleeping claim in hopes of spying beaver during the night. We won't see any, but loud tail slaps will startle us awake more than once.

Darkness arrives suddenly. As we sit around a fire, our bellies full of pasta, Stan tells the story behind the island's name. In the mid-1800s, a man named Woody made a name for himself by opening a saloon on the Willamette's west bank, a couple miles north of present-day Junction City. Soon enough people gathered in and around his saloon that the area was known as Woodyville, also the location of a navigation port that Woody and his family operated. On account of his reputation for hardscrabble toughness, Woody dispensed a local distillation commonly known as Blue Ruin. He lived his reputation well, with a large and unwholesome family who competed with other navigation companies through bullying, intimidation, and even sabotage.

I want to listen more, but the grogginess that comes with exhaustion visits me at closer and closer intervals. Everyone else is silent too, heads resting on hands and eyes trying to stay open after an entire day of paddling.

My friend and I head toward our plateau near the beaver superhighway. Above, the Big Dipper ladles a scoop of darkness, spoiled only by a beam of moonlight flickering under clouds. We have been out of the water for hours, but somehow, even in stillness, I feel the river's gentle rush and rock around me. The power of its sway grows wide. So wide that I can no longer tell where it began.

9/21/2010

My alarm startles me awake. My fingers are swollen from the heat of my sleeping bag, and my brain is foggy from the open cold. I get up and shake off my bag. "I swear I heard a beaver chewing willow sticks right by my head," I say to my friend.

She replies, "I could almost hear them walking right by us." Sure enough, fresh tracks pit the beaver superhighway.

It's 7:30 a.m. and we are packed and dressed, which turns out to be easy because we wear the same things we slept in. Walking toward the group, we are surprised to see most everyone awake and huddled around a fire with thermoses in hand. The nearby air smells of wet duff, fire smoke, and coffee. People talk about what they hope to do after school, while Stan and Randy share stories of research trips on the river and gear they lost to the current. It will be another hour before we clean everything up and get on the river again.

Today I sit on the other side of the boat so I don't burden my already-sore muscles from yesterday. I'm with a different group of people and a new guide—the same fisheries and wildlife student who showed me how to knot the raft strap.

116

Our first stop is a large gravel bar along the banks of a small town called Harrisburg. Where the gravel bar meets the shore is a stranded boat ramp. The city installed the ramp to improve river access, but over time the Willamette deposited a swath of stones and blocked the ramp. We talk about what the city could do to regain river access. They could mine the gravel bar and use it for concrete. They could dredge it and deposit it elsewhere. But the river would just bring it back. Often we treat systems as symptoms. Symptoms can be "cured" but a system cannot—at least not entirely. Deposition of gravel is part of a system and just something a river does.

We can, however, interfere with the system. Stan tells us that summer flows are now 2 to 2.5 times higher than historic flows. The Army Corps holds water back during the wet months and releases it during the warm months. In addition, one river mile today along the area we are floating was around five to six miles before settlement, on account of the river's meanders.

We can only interfere so much before the river says enough, which is what happened with Harrisburg's boat ramp. The town might be inconvenienced by a land-locked ramp, but the shallow water by the gravel bar can be great habitat for juvenile Chinook salmon, says Kirk Schroeder with the Oregon Department of Fish and Wildlife. He, along with Michael Pope from the Greenbelt Land Trust and Steve Horning, the young farmer of Deerhaven Farms I interviewed, will accompany us along the next stretch of river.

❖ ❖ ❖

The day flickers between sun and grey, and in a similar fashion, the shoreline changes from forty-foot willows and ash to areas cleared for farmland. One inside bend is covered with bright green grass with the long necks of heron sticking out like spy scopes. The next is a row of Christmas tree crops overhanging a steep bank, with roots clinging to the sandy soil. Throughout this stretch we see distinct layers of soil and rock in the bank and learn that the very bottom layer is likely from the

Missoula Floods, the same floods that deposited "erratic" rocks on Dave Buchanan's land. Geologically speaking, it is possible to go back in time.

We're not on the water long before pulling out to eat a lunch. With food in hand, we circle around Steve Horning. Steve has an easy manner about him, answering any and every question we throw his way. His well-kept hair and collared shirt give him more of the look of a college-boy than a farmer, which might be from the time he spent at Western Oregon University and Oregon State University before coming back to the family farm.

Restoration, Steve tells us, can mean losing productive property to the river. Reconnect a channel, and it may flood the land. Remove the riprap, and the river could migrate and take out trees. But more than that, planting native vegetation can send unwanted seeds downstream that infiltrate adjacent fields. Restoration can reduce the tax base and require costly adjustments for farmers, such as repositioning their irrigation system. The permitting process can be long. Dozens of agencies can be involved. Years can pass before any of the restoration work begins.

But I don't want to paint Steve as an anti-restorationist. Far from it. Deerhaven Farms is working with Greenbelt Land Trust to restore 320 acres near Harkins Lake. "We believe that it only makes sense to benefit the environment and your pocket book at the same time," he says.

Steve says that scientists survey fish by the farm twice a year, but he has never been surveyed. No one has taken the time to ask his opinion or hear from his family, a family who has watched the river change for one hundred years. His comment struck me, and maybe all of us in the class. Restoration is so often framed as an ecological issue, but it's easy for people with scientific leanings to forget that it's a social one as well. The work is not just about fish but farmers too. There are more strands knotted together than I ever imagined.

❖ ❖ ❖

We finish the day by paddling down to Irish Bend, our final destination. In a flurry of movement, we deflate the rafts, roll them up, and haul them into a white van. Tonight, we'll stay in Corvallis, which for me and other OSU students means we'll be sleeping in our own beds. I let my shoulders down at the thought. My ass is wet and arms are tired. The night before I had slept on soft river grit and drifted into a dreamstate punctuated by beaver tail slaps. Tonight, I fall asleep next to Ben. The only sound between us is the slow cadence of our breath, each one becoming something more imagined than real.

9/22/2010

Ten hours later. I'm in the white van again with companions who are becoming more familiar each day. They are no longer outlines of people who study landscape architecture and enjoy gardening, but people who are asking intelligent questions about the place they live. How can we pull back our infrastructure and let the river breathe? Why aren't more salmon swimming up the Willamette River and migrating into coastal streams? How *do* you restore a big big river like the Willamette?

We begin the day's journey at Hyak Park near Albany, where we meet two new guests, Pam Wiley, with Meyer Memorial Trust, and Paula Burgess, with Oregon Watershed Enhancement Board. This time we set up the rafts with laughter and jokes, despite our tiredness. For the third time, I hear the story about a student falling out of the boat on the first day, and a group of us laugh in remembrance. We haul gear out of the vans by forming a line and passing along equipment like a human conveyor belt. The rest is familiar: we pick a paddle and a life vest; we carry inflated rafts down to the water, along with our day bags and coolers; and then we gather to hear introductions from our new guests.

Pam and Paula launch into a discussion about restoration on the mainstem Willamette, an area that until recently has been avoided. Not because of apathy. The mainstem is simply a huge river with a lot of power. In addition, some projects, like channel reconnections, require complex and expensive modeling intended to determine how rivers behave over space and time. Facing the group with the catcher's mitts of bigleaf maple leaves pawing his head, Stan asks the group: Can one model measure how a channel reconnection will affect birds, terrestrial species, etc, over many, many years? His question suggests a need for adaptive management—that we stay responsive and flexible to a changing system, that we monitor our data to assess whether our predictive potential for change can be confirmed or refuted, that we acknowledge uncertainty when history is limited or the desired conditions differ greatly from those of the past. The adage "all models are wrong; some models are useful" rings true. It is phrased more eloquently by Professor Don Falk: "How can we fully understand the forces that move deserts, melt ice caps, elevate sea level, build mountains, float continents, and cause species to emerge and disappear like so many fireflies on a summer night? Some humility is in order here."

Then Stan talks about something I have never thought of. He suggests letting the river do some of the work and giving it freedom to self restore, where appropriate. We can bring in the backhoes and lengthen an alcove, but sometimes the river might be able to lengthen itself. The river is a participant in restoration, too.

The group fidgets. Some sit, shift position, cock one hip and then the other. For my part, I'm ready to be on the water again. It's already 11 a.m.

The current along the middle stretch dabbles rather than drums, half unfamiliar from its quickened pace above Harrisburg. In a way, there are rivers within rivers, disaccord and change between reaches, permutations of patterns becoming something new. The whole world can change in a few paddle strokes. Pay attention: farms become fields of cottonwoods, bridges span concrete banks. Look sharp: a palatial home gives way to an empty osprey nest on top of a telephone pole.

This stretch I'm in the boat with Dave Hulse, the other instructor from the University of Oregon. The students are content to let him tell story after story about the river and surrounding people. One story sticks with me, and I have already retold it many times. As we pass Bryant Park where the Calapooia River comes in, Dave points to a clearing. Until recently, one hundred fifty-year-old cottonwoods stood there

(Randy counted the rings). Dave, Stan, and Randy surmise that the floods in the 1860s laid down the cottonwood seeds. The high waters that ripped through the valley and destroyed property also created something new: a patchwork of saplings that grew and watched Albany expand over the years. They saw the introduction of the railroad, the remaining Natives shoved aside for progress, and the slow atrophy of a river choked by progress. It's amazing that something we consider so destructive can also bring renewal. But all the history wrapped in those one hundred fifty-year-old trees died when the city decided they were a hazard and cut them down. If we had passed by the clearing at Bryant Park without the story of the cottonwoods, I would have mistaken it for a simple patch of grass.

Stories of landscapes bring meaning to our lives. Before the advent of written communication, before books and blogs, people told oral histories, crafted and recited in place. Now, our stories are traded across countries. They grow in one place and are told or read somewhere far away. There is nothing wrong with globalizing our stories through written language, but I think it's important to learn about the stories under our feet. Those stories have special meaning. The hill in our backyard or brook running through town has a unique genesis. Learning the history behind the local natural world attaches meaning to the places we experience daily, until that hill or brook become something more than a namesake. They become woven into our lives as ongoing characters in our narrative.

❖ ❖ ❖

We eat lunch on an island and listen more to Pam and Paula. They are truly champions of the Willamette. They go through the exhausting permitting, planning, approval, and funding process of restoring the mainstem. My head spins with all the acronyms and approval boards, grantees, agencies, and advocacy organizations involved in the restoration process. They talk about the difficulty of planning on the mainstem Willamette, an account of city infrastructure and homes so close to the bank. They talk about overcoming lingering mistrust from the agricultural community stemming from the Willamette Greenway Program. Where urbanites and environmentalists generally saw the program as a triumph for protecting river bottomlands, some landowners with holdings near the river saw it as an underhanded attempt by the government to snatch up land and restrict farming practices.

With all the challenges and red tape, I start wondering how any project ever gets approved, or whether restoration risks being co-opted by bureaucracy. Of course we *need* professionals and practitioners, but we also need people. We need ordinary citizens to care. Restoration may be less of a technical issue than an ethical one, at least fundamentally, because it means committing ourselves to something we value and what those values require of us. We need people to see the river as a character in the stories we create. No regulatory process can ensure an ethic of environmental responsibility.

Maybe Pam and Paula pick up on my doubt. How do we begin? I keep asking myself. How do we fight this fight? When there are so many people, agencies, and politics involved, how does restoration not become a tangled, snarled mess? More than once, Pam and Paula say they need people like us. They need people who are starting careers to continue the work of Team Willamette. The work is slow and continuous. It's never easy or perfect, but we have to try. In the end, that's all we can do—accept the imperfections of bringing together the frayed strands of restoration and keep trying.

❖❖❖

We arrive at Luckiamute Landing with just enough sunlight to unload and set up tents. Near the shore, two students sit cross-legged and meditate facing the river. Two others skip stones. And two upright paddles tent a pair of wet pants. On the nearside of east, the sun crawls towards the horizon, and a spider creeps steadily over uneven stones. In this moment, I'm overcome by an intense desire to understand why people love water so much, even those who aren't river rats or fish squeezers. Oregon naturalist Robin Cody writes that all the willows, beaver, and other water dwellers are just another way the river carries itself through the vessels of other beings—stems and bones slurping up water. But I wonder if the opposite is true—that the water in our cells and veins are called by the river, back to the primordial pool that birthed us. Our blood might have the same root composition of water formed in the days when wetness was our home. Our former life as a fish haunts us, something atavistic and ancient recessed in our guts. Even though people can no longer survive in water, our legs may remember when they were fins. We have long since abandoned the salty seas for earth, but the underwater world still calls to us.

❖❖❖

As the sun fades we gather around a picnic table and fire pit, giving ourselves time to take in all that we have learned throughout the day. Paula plays Frisbee with a few students, while another group circles up and talks about how to make the best margarita. Night falls gently and carries the smell of wood smoke and charcoal grill. Stan and Dave are making burgers and hotdogs, and they cook for the entire group without complaint.

We are content to stand around the fire with our food, as light from the near-full moon haloes our heads. We take turns reading from a book of poems and become more theatric as the bravery and beer settle in. A few students roast marshmallows on willow sticks, trying to see who can get the perfect browned skin without charring it. Laughs, groans, and sighs rise in time with embers that spark against an onyx sky. Tomorrow will be our final day on the Willamette.

9/23/2010

Either from weariness or eagerness to be home, the group is quiet today. The rain doesn't help. It smatters our coats in generous dollops. Somehow we can withstand the water splashing from below but not above. My "rainproof" jacket has soaked through and a cold I can't shake settles in deep. I try to think back to only a few weeks ago, when I was so hot I could barely stand it, but the feeling is too distant to seem real.

After a quick stop for lunch on a less-than-ideal shoreline, we paddle straight for Independence. The guides point out different landmarks: the Buena Vista Ferry, sandstone walls that look to be one hundred feet tall. In my boat, we acknowledge these landmarks with a brief, "Ah yes," or "Hmmm," more out of courtesy than interest. Despite the windburn on my face and the exhaustion in my bones, I sit in front and set the pace of one stroke per second. The woman on the other side keeps my rhythm. We hardly break except to wipe the rain from our faces.

On land again, we pack everything up with the intensity of worker bees: cleaning out the rafts, deflating them, gathering paddles, stacking life jackets, hauling, loading, separating. The group circles around one last time, close enough to appear chainlinked together. After the cramp of tents and rafts, we feel at ease standing near one another. The final gathering is brief and unadorned. We give our thanks, and then we go home.

As a final class requirement, each of us submits a reflection on the trip. I could have written about the policy of restoration or the science. I could have shared my doubts and opinions on whether it's all feasible. Instead, I share my hope. I hope that we stay connected to this place and remember the sway of the Willamette. And I hope that we understand restoration is as much about the land as it is about our hearts and minds.

I had good reason for that hope. All of a sudden, a flood of responses came from other students, full of wonder and gratitude. They wrote about learning from past generations, about enjoying, cherishing, and honoring the resources we have to pass along a healthier river system. They wrote about feeling closer to farmers and land. They asked what their own role might be in the future and the slow threading of relationships to fulfill the necessary work. One student wrote about her newfound understanding of the phrase, *we're all in the same boat*, feeling the connection between the "raft, the river, and us." And one wrote about how the course of her life had been altered, as if the world suddenly dropped a big boulder in her stream and sent her in a new direction.

We got out of the boat and still cared. We could easily undo the knotted strands, just by tugging the end and walking away. We could go back to being undone, calling the weight of loss too great and look with pity to the future, having never grasped the courage to imagine a world better than the one we inherited. It would be easy to do.

Or we could remember the fin of fish cutting upstream, the bone and beak of heron, the fertile farmland, the larkspur, turtle, fox, and the volunteer; the agency and the visionary, the engineer and the owl. We might remember that the world is woven. "When one tugs at a single thing in nature, he finds it attached to the rest of the world," says John Muir. How do we continue, then, to make this daily braid?

❖ ❖ ❖

At home on solid land, after I've unpacked and warmed up, I find a strap I use to harness my kayak to the car. As best I can, I remember the instructions from the fisheries and wildlife student on the first day, which seems far away. You make a loop, and then another loop. I take the straight strand and make loops, weaving each one through the previous circle. Somehow I remember the swish of his hands. When I am done, my strap is woven. It's imperfect and warped with uneven bulges, but knotted just the same.

Meander Scars

❖❖❖

"When a doctor sets a broken arm, he just holds the pieces in place with a splint and nature does the rest ... Likewise with restoration: It is more like being a midwife than being an artist or engineer"
—Holmes Rolston III

A leaf-littered path veers into an arch of broadleaf trees and conifers. The Oregon ash stand solemn with bare branches; the oaks—both Oregon white and California black—wave lichen-bearded limbs; and the Doug-fir bow under the weight of rain. The snowberries have pushed out their first pearls, but most everything else is de-leafed and twigged. Even the sky looks bare. Instead of a low winter sun wreathing the sky, a depthless grey extends from hill to horizon.

I am walking in the twenty-three hundred-acre Howard Buford Recreation Area between the confluence of the Coast and Middle Forks of the Willamette River. Here, volunteers have been working for years to enhance floodplain habitat within a two-hundred-acre region called

South Meadow. I have come to see a recent channel excavation and reconnection project, to see what it looks like to build a river.

The path to South Meadow curls from a crowded parking lot and through rain-slicked trees with licorice ferns draped from the trunks. Then, it runs parallel to the Coast Fork before opening up to a field where cattle grazed for many years. It is here that the Friends of Buford Park & Mt. Pisgah are trying to bring back native vegetation, in addition to reconnecting old river channels still ringed with trees.

I stop to look at the Coast Fork to get a sense of its mood. Brown water churns as though it has somewhere to be. At the far shore, bare willows stalks have turned blood red, the only color in this two-toned afternoon, except for small washes of green from Himalayan blackberries. Further back, the upper branches of broadleaf trees reach upward like a river delta yearning for the sea.

The noise of other people falls away. Soon, the only human sound is the crunch of my boots on gravel, gravel that has been pried loose by thin fingers of water grasping for the Willamette. I'm not sure I'm going the right way. It doesn't help when I don't see another soul around and hear the whispering *tsk* of kinglets above my head. *Tsk tsk,* they say. *Silly girl. You're going the wrong way.* The weight of a distant place sinks in further when I read a nearby sign: *Not a designated swimming area. Deep water. Sometimes polluted. Swim at your own risk.* For the third time in a quarter mile, I get out my map to see how far I am from South Meadow. By now the map is haloed with water droplets and the lacy pattern of running ink. I promise myself I won't deviate from the trail, even to look at the river.

I had planned to meet someone out here, a man named Chris Orsinger. Chris is the executive director of the Friends of Buford Park and orchestrator of the South Meadow project. He would have made an excellent guide, but the week before Christmas turned out to be too busy for him. I had met Chris at a Willamette River conference, where we talked about the South Meadow project. He was late for a workshop but talked to me anyway, pulling out maps and laminated images of the area, answering all my questions without pause or impatience. In one aerial photo of South Meadow during the 1996 flood, Chris showed me how the high water filled historic side channels of the Coast Fork. Under normal flow, water no longer fills these channels because they've been blocked by culverts and rock pilings. What are left are dry, shallow depressions that Chris called "meander scars."

My mind flashed. I kept nodding and smiling as Chris talked, looking perfectly attentive. But my head was somewhere else. In scientific and restoration circles, phrases like *lateral channel migration, fluvial dynamics, benthic invertebrates,* and *nonstructural flood storage* are common. But *meander scars* was so ... plain? Harsh? Unkind? What did it mean? Scars are leftovers of harm, the body's attempt at wound repair, some cruel reminder of hurt, some evidence that a thing used to be broken. The phrase implies that the river was the wound, and the absence of it the scar. It wouldn't surprise me if people saw rivers as an injury that needs fixing, considering the Swiss-German word for channelization is "corrected," as if rivers were intrinsically broken and needed our intervention to heal.

I don't think Chris meant *meander scars* in this way. I think he used it to refer to what's left over from *our* harm, because we have injured rivers in many ways. Maybe reconnecting what we have severed is one way to undo this harm.

After meeting Chris, I looked at aerial photos of the river near my home, curious to see these meander scars. They were everywhere, scored into fields and crops. Then they would sigh into a faint shadow, like a chocked-off thought. Here and there, blue lines of river faded to a hollow wrinkle. I realized the slight depressions on Ed Rust's property were indeed the meander scars of the Little Willamette.

I wanted to see these scars up close.

Which is why I'm out at South Meadow now. The area just before the meadow doesn't look like a place of healing or repair. It looks like a combat zone. Piles of wood, both cut from trees and milled, scatter the ground. As I walk by, a Pacific wren springs from a wood pile, bobs, and then calls in warning. All around is evidence of intervention: a pile of mulch and earthmover tracks cradling small pools of rainwater. When I enter the open field of South Meadow, stakes, flags, and a waterlogged glove are scattered about among the brush.

Restoration is sometimes a paradox. Well-intentioned people inflict wounds to heal the scars of a past injury, similar to when doctors break a bone on purpose so it heals right. The hope is the temporary invasion will lead to greater recovery, that the original scars will fade, and that the system will work as it did before. Sometimes the body can't heal itself without intervention, and maybe the land works this way, too.

Often I've feared that the wounds we make in the name of healing could be too deep for the land to recover from, especially when I think of Ben and an injury he suffered as a nineteen-year-old. While remodeling a house, he cut his right hand on a skilsaw, severing the tendons in his thumb and index finger. The gash was atrocious. Even when doctors dressed the wound and Ben elevated his hand, blood trailed down his forearm, draining from the severed network of vessels. When they finally sewed him up, jagged black stitches threaded down his hand. It looked like Frankenstein. I remember seeing Ben stare at it, his face ashen.

The worst of his scars, however, were not from the skilsaw, but from the doctors. When Ben severed his tendons, they snapped down to his wrists. The doctors had to cut into his palm to get to the tendons and reconnect them. Now the wrinkled edge of a scar runs the length of his palm, fading into the skin of his wrist. And he never recovered full function and sensation of his index finger and thumb. Every winter, a deep cold plagues his hand. The blood doesn't flow right, even with everything connected again. It's the slow accumulation of scar tissue. Doctors have suggested further surgeries to remove the tissue and improve his circulation. But Ben decided to let his hand do the rest of the healing. He didn't want any more intervention.

Rivers don't have scar tissue, but they have silt. And silt could build up and block the water from flowing.

❖❖❖

I come to a lookout point at a wetland and excavated channel. Mesh netting has been laid down along the bank, possibly to prevent erosion and allow plants to establish. From what I can tell from my map, this area was excavated some years ago. The plan was to open up the channel again to improve water quality and fish passage, allowing the area's network of veins to circulate water. Aside from the mesh netting, the channel looks real. Snarled branches tangle the shore. Leaves are underwater too—yellow, orange, flaming red, and the white undersides of willow leaves. I blur my eyes, and the netting disappears. Even when my eyes are back in focus, I could almost overlook it with the throaty sound of water moving over rocks and distracting my vision.

Further along, the South Meadow trail bends to a channel that was excavated only a few months ago. Unlike the one I just passed, the channel has denuded banks and a steep grade that run for several yards. Stakes with bright orange tips rise from the middle of the water. Black fabric stretches across the channel, crumpled in places like dirty laundry. Netting crosshatches the ground. The trees and shrubs are gone. The wound still gapes. When I pull out the excavation plans I see that even the logs and deep pools were deliberately placed, a level of precision that makes South Meadow seem prosthetic rather than a step toward healing.

In the rain I turn my head down and stare, not at any particular point. Eyes and mind un-focus, trailing into a half dream, half aware of the rain, and feeling the cold more within than without.

Maybe the unsettling cold is because in addition to the netting, the fabric, and the absence of trees, I don't see any aquatic insects when I overturn stone after stone. Maybe because I know for every South Meadow story there are a thousand other scars that will remain, or wounds that will never heal.

It's odd to think that people would even try to fix something as complex as a river—this endless story of a stream, flowing on and on, and never pausing for a moment. Think where the water has traveled. It slid through soil and pockets of air, passing through worms and moistening a stone. It traveled through the downy throat of a fawn, moving into its gut. The water climbed through stems and gave the nootka roses its petals. The water twisted in the trunks of oak trees and slid down the knotted skin of cottonwoods. It lifted into the air and came down as rain onto mountains, slowly softening their edges. It leaned into the earth—deep—where it stayed cool and then mixed back in with the water of the stream. Yet we pretend to know how to fix something that traveled through sky and earth, and so many places in between.

But then my mood turns sympathetic. The Friends of Buford Park have sowed and pulled on behalf of a river. They have logged more hours than I could imagine and undertaken not just the simple tasks of removing species and bringing back others. They have done more than plant trees and pull weeds. They are rebuilding a river, and how brave of them to do it. How unfair of me to criticize something as a spectator. Perhaps the risk of greater injury is worth the possibility of healing. Plus, haven't I complained about the philosophers who view restoration as a human-created fakery?

The meadow will take time to mend. The grass and trees have yet to grow back and heal the earthmovers' scrape. For some time, stitches of netting will score this flat palm of land. The water has just begun to flow from the winter rain and will take time to pump through all river veins. Silt could build up and reduce circulation. But for now, it is time to let the river do the work. No more surgeries. Let the rain fall, and let the water run.

At my final stop, I come to a seasonal crossing with low grade, now full with ankle-high water. Chris warned me about this spot—if it rains heavily enough and the water rises fast, I might not be able to cross and get back safely. I might have to climb a tree, he said. The rain has stopped, so I feel safe to stand in the middle of the crossing and let the water smack against my rubber boots.

I blur my eyes but I still don't see trees. The netting and fabric smear to a haze but don't disappear. So I close my eyes completely. Everything fades. In my waking dream, the prints of Caterpillar tractors become fox and turtle. The trees and understory shrubs grow back in my mind's eye. I can picture the wicker pattern of branches and twigs near the

132

soft water. Then the faintest sound, like a small tap, reaches my ears. I imagine a lingering oak leaf trilling the water's surface.

Can this channel ever be whole again? Will these meander scars fade into the imagination and hope of a wild river, the one in my head and heart?

This much I know: Ben's hand isn't the same as it was, and it never will be again. But when it reaches for mine, it feels like love. And right now, the water at South Meadow is flowing. It fills in the shadowed trench that presses into the earth. It flows and bends around the streambed curves. When I touch it, it feels like a river.

Bibliography

(with a few annotations for more information)

Abbot, Carl (2004). A century of change. In *The Oregon History Project*. Retrieved from http://www.ohs.org/the-oregon-history-project/narratives/lewis-and-clark/lewis-and-clark-centennial-exposition/century-change.cfm

Alexandersson, O. (2002). *Living Water. Viktor Schauberger and the Secrets of Natural Energy* (2nd ed.). Green Forest, AR: Newleaf Publishing Group.

Alt, D., and D. W. Hyndman (1981). *Roadside Geology of Oregon* (2nd ed.). Missoula, MT: Mountain Press Publishing Co.

Associated Press (1881, January 28). The flood! Reports from Corvallis, Salem, Oregon City, Albany, and other places in the Valley. *Eugene City Guard*. Retrieved from http://news.google.com/newspapers?id=hUtXAAA AIBAJ&sjid-9u8D AAAAIBAJ&pg=6212,622248&dq=the-flood-reports-from-corvallis&hl=en

Associated Press (1943, January 4). Nine Oregonians die in Willamette flood. *Los Angeles Times*, pp. 1A, 2A.

Associated Press (1964, December 27). Worst appears to be over. *Eugene Register-Guard*, p. 1A.

Bauer, W. S. (1980). *A case analysis of Oregon's Willamette River Greenway Program*. (Unpublished doctoral dissertation). Oregon State University, Corvallis. Bauer's dissertation is an excellent summary of the Willamette Greenway Program's genesis, its major players, and perceived success. Citing tensions between agricultural communities and supporters, as well as the challenges in coordinating various political jurisdictions, the author concludes that the program has been a limited success at best.

Benner, P. Personal communication, May 11, 2010.

Benner, P. (2009). *The Willamette River near Corvallis: River History and Ecology*. Corvallis, OR. Self published.

Benner, P. A., and J. R. Sedell (1997). Upper Willamette River landscape: A historic perspective. In A. Laenen and D. A. Dunnette (eds.), *River Quality: Dynamics and Restoration* (pp. 23-49). New York: CRC Press, Inc.

Bennett, M. (2007). Managing Himalayan blackberry in western Oregon riparian areas. *Oregon State University Extension Management, 8894*. Retrieved from http://extension.oregonstate.edu/catalog/pdf/em/em8894.pdf

Binus, J. (2004). Beaver trap. In *The Oregon History Project*. Retrieved from http://www.ohs.org/education/oregonhistory/historical_records/ dspDocument.cfm?doc_ID=66620F05-0E60-BE11-791565100325BC72

Black, L. D. (1940). *Willamette River history: The peopling of the middle Willamette Valley*. (Unpublished doctoral dissertation). University of Michigan, Ann Arbor.

Branscomb, A. (2002). Geology. In D. Hulse, S. Gregory and J. Baker (eds.), *Willamette River Basin Atlas: Trajectories of Environmental and Ecological Change*. Retrieved from http://www.fsl.orst.edu/pnwerc/wrb/Atlas_web_ compressed/PDFtoc.html

Camp, C. L. (ed.). (1960). *James Clyman, Frontiersman; The Adventures of a Trapper and Covered-wagon Emigrant as Told in His Own Reminiscences and Diaries*. Champoeg, OR: The Champoeg Press.

Carson, K. Personal communication, June 14, 2010.

City of Portland (2012, August 1). Development along the Willamette River. Retrieved from http://www.portlandonline.com/bes/index. cfm?a=231478&c=30938

Clark, R. C. (1927). *History of the Willamette Valley, Oregon*. Chicago, IL: The S.J. Clarke Publishing Company.

Corning, H. M. (2004). *Willamette Landings* (3rd ed.). Portland: Oregon Historical Society Press.

Dykaar, B. B., and P. J. Wigington, Jr. (2000). Floodplain formation and cottonwood colonization patterns on the Willamette River, Oregon, USA. *Environmental Management*, 25(1), 87-104.

Falk, D. (1990). Discovering the future, creating the past: Some reflections on restoration. *Restoration & Management Noes*, 8(2), 71-72.

Fletcher, R. (2007). *Willamette Valley Ponderosa Pine: A Primer*. Retrieved from http://www.westernforestry.org/wvppca/2008/ WillametteValleyPonderosaPinePrimer2007.pdf

Green, S. Personal communication, June 21, 2010.

Gregory, S. Personal communication, May 4, 2011.

Gregory, S. V. (2008). Historical channel modification and floodplain forest decline: Implications for conservation and restoration of a large floodplain river – the Willamette River, Oregon. In H. Habersack, H. Piégay, and M. Rinaldi (eds.), *Gravel-bed River VI: From Process Understanding to River Restoration* (pp. 763-75). Amsterdam, The Netherlands: Elsevier.

Gregory, S., et al. (2002a). Flood inundations/ FEMA floodplains. In D. Hulse, S. Gregory and J. Baker (eds.), *Willamette River Basin Atlas: Trajectories of Environmental and Ecological Change*. Retrieved from http://www.fsl.orst. edu/pnwerc/wrb/Atlas_web_compressed/PDFtoc.html.

Gregory, S., et al. (2002b). Presettlement Vegetation ca. 1851. In D. Hulse, S. Gregory and J. Baker (eds.), *Willamette River Basin Atlas: Trajectories of Environmental and Ecological Change*. Retrieved from http://www.fsl.orst.edu/pnwerc/wrb/Atlas_web_compressed/PDFtoc.html .

Gregory, S., et al. (2002c). Fish assemblages. In D. Hulse, S. Gregory & J. Baker (Eds.), *Willamette River Basin Atlas: Trajectories of Environmental and Ecological Change*. Retrieved from http://www.fsl.orst.edu/pnwerc/wrb/Atlas_web_compressed/PDFtoc.html

Hall, B. (2011, January 16). Farmers make a stand. *Corvallis Gazette-Times*. Retrieved from http://gazettetimes.com/article_24e57eeb-dc56-5260-b3db_012b0f631785.html

House, F. (2000). *Totem Salmon: Life Lessons from Another Species*. Boston, MA: Beacon Press.

Howell, E. A., J. A. Harrington, and S. B. Glass (2012). *Introduction to Restoration Ecology*. Washington, DC: Island Press.

Hynes, H. B. N. (1970). *The Ecology of Running Waters*. Liverpool, UK: Liverpool University Press.

Juntunen, J. R., M. D. Dasch, and A.B. Rogers (2005). *The World of the Kalapuya: A Native people of Western Oregon*. Philomath, OR: Benton County Historical Society and Museum.

Katz, E. (2000). The big lie: Human restoration of nature. In Throop, W. (ed.), *Environmental Restoration: Ethics, Theory, and Practice* (pp. 83-93). New York: Humanity Books.

Kittredge, W. (2007). Owning it all. In *The Next Rodeo: New and Selected Essays* (pp. 51-66). Saint Paul, MN.: Graywolf Press.

Klingeman, P. C. (1987). Proceedings from the Corvallis Symposium: *Erosion and Sedimentation in the Pacific Rim*. Corvallis, OR. Retrieved from http://iahs.info/redbooks/a165/iahs_165_0365.pdf

Lampman, B. H. (1946). *The Coming of the Pond Fishes*. Portland, OR: Binfords & Mort.

Leopold, A. (1949). *A Sand County Almanac, and Sketches Here and There*. New York: Oxford University Press.

Leopold, A. (1953). *Round River: From the Journals of Aldo Leopold*. New York: Oxford University Press.

Light, A. (2000). Restoration or domination? A reply to Katz. In Throop, W. (ed.), *Environmental Restoration: Ethics, Theory, and Practice* (pp. 95-111). New York: Humanity Books. Marsh, G. P. (1965). *Man and Nature*. Cambridge, MA: Belknap Press of Harvard University Press.

Maser, C. (2009). *Earth in Our Care: Ecology, Economy, and Sustainability*. Piscataway, NJ: Rutgers University Press.

McArthur, L. A. (2003). *Oregon Geographic Names* (7th ed.). Seattle: University of Washington Press.

Mills, S. (1995). *In Service of the Wild: Restoring and Reinhabiting Damaged Land.* Boston, MA: Beacon Press.

Mockford, J. (2005). Before Lewis and Clark, Lt. Broughton's river of names: The Columbia River exploration of 1792. *Oregon Historical Quarterly, 106*(4), 542-67.

Mullane, N. (1997). The Willamette River of Oregon: A river restored? In A. Laenen and D. A. Dunnette (eds.), *River Quality: Dynamics and Restoration* (pp. 65-75). New York: CRC Press, Inc. This chapter provides an overview of cleanup efforts on the Willamette, beginning in the late 1930s and continuing through the 1960s and '70s. As a result of citizen concern and a growing consciousness of the Willamette's poor water quality, the river's health was drastically improved, and its cleanup has been hailed as a national success. Governor Tom McCall is often credited for spearheading the cleanup (with his famous documentary *Pollution in Paradise* and broad support of environmental initiatives), although efforts began well before his tenure as governor (1967-1975). For example, in the 1930s, Oregonians passed a referendum to create the state's first sewage treatment plants. Today, pollution sources are much more elusive. Rather than raw sewage coming from a direct source (known as a point-source pollution), the Willamette contends with non-point source pollutants from agricultural runoff, residential lawn care, and heavy metals from construction sites. For an overview of pollution on the Willamette, read James Hillegas' master's thesis from Portland State University (2009): *Working for the 'Working River': Willamette River Pollution, 1926-1962.*

Nabhan, G. P. (1990. Restoring and re-storying the landscape. *Restoration and Management Notes, 9*(1), 3-4.

Oetter, D. R., et al. (2004). GIS methodology for characterizing historical conditions of the Willamette River flood plain, Oregon. *Transactions in GIS, 8*(3), 367-83.

Oliver, M. (2010). For example. In *Swan: Poems and Prose Poems* (pp. 11-12). Boston, MA: Beacon Press.

Oregon Department of Agriculture, Noxious Weed Control (2009). *Armenian blackberry (Himalayan).* Retrieved from http://www.oregon.gov/ODA/PLANT/WEEDS/profile_himalayanblackberry.shtml

Osterkamp, W. R. (1998). Processes of fluvial island formation, with examples from Plum Creek, Colorado and Snake River, Idaho. *Society of Wetland Scientists, 18*(4), 530-45.

Payne, S., and J. Baker (2002). Introduction: Study area. In D. Hulse, S. Gregory and J. Baker (eds.), *Willamette River Basin Atlas: Trajectories of Environmental and Ecological Change.* Retrieved from http://www.fsl.orst.edu/pnwerc/wrb/Atlas_web_compressed/PDFtoc.html .

Pope, M. Personal communication, July 20, 2010.

Richey, D. (2002). Land ownership. In D. Hulse, S. Gregory and J. Baker (eds.), *Willamette River Basin Atlas: Trajectories of Environmental and Ecological Change.* Retrieved from http://www.fsl.orst.edu/pnwerc/wrb/Atlas_web_compressed/PDFtoc.html .

Robbins, W. G. (1978). The Willamette Valley Project of Oregon: A study in the political economy of resource development. *Pacific Historical Review, 47*, 585-605.

Rolston, H. (1994). *Conserving Natural Value.* New York: Columbia University Press.

Sanches, J. Personal communication, August 29, 2010.Schweickert, T. Personal communication, Feb 6, 2012.

Sedell, J. R., and J. L. Froggatt (1984). Importance of streamside forests to large rivers: The isolation of the Willamette River, Oregon, U.S.A., from its floodplain by snagging and streamside forest removal. *Verh. Internat. Verin. Limnol, 22*, 1828-34.

Throop, W, and R. Purdom (2006) Wilderness restoration: The paradox of public participation. *Restoration Ecology, 14*(4), 493-99. This article covers the contradictions and challenges of inviting the public to participate in restoration, particularly in wilderness areas, and provides a broader discussion of the topics touched on in *Trees, Weeds, and Rivers.*

St. John, P., and I. Wendt (eds.). (1993). *From Here We Speak: An Anthology of Oregon Poetry.* Corvallis: Oregon State University Press.

United States Department of Agriculture. (2009). Web soil survey [Data file]. Retrieved from http://websoilsurvey.nrcs.usda.gov/app/WebSoilSurvey.aspx

Van Wieren, G. (2008). Ecological restoration as public spiritual practice. *Worldviews, 12*, 237-54.

Vancouver, G. (1926). *The Exploration of the Columbia River, 1792: An Extract from the Journal of Captain George Vancouver.* Longview, WA: from the press of the *Daily News.*

Wallick, J. R., et al.. (2007). Patterns and controls on historical channel change in the Willamette River, Oregon, USA. In A. Gupta (ed.), *Large Rivers: Geomorphology and Management* (pp. 491-516). Hoboken, NJ: John Wiley & Sons, Ltd.

Willamette Riverkeeper (2008). *Mission Bottom channel restoration*. Retrieved
from http://www.willamette-riverkeeper.org/WRK/documents/mission-
bottom-channel-restoration.pdf

Local Resources

General Information
Map of Oregon Watersheds
  http://cms.oregon.gov/OWEB/pages/watershed_council_contacts.aspx
The Oregon Encyclopedia
  http://www.oregonencyclopedia.org/entry/view/willamette_river/
Willamette Basin Explorer
  http://www.willametteexplorer.info/
Willamette River History
  http://www.portlandonline.com/bes/index.cfm?a=231478&c=30938

Reports and Publications
Agriculture Water Quality Management Plans
  http://oregon.gov/ODA/NRD/pages/water_agplans.aspx
Bowers Rock State Park Channel Reconnection
  http://www.willamette-riverkeeper.org/WRK/documents/bowers-rock-
  reconnection-project.pdf
Integrated Water Management Strategy
  http://www.oregon.gov/owrd/pages/law/integrated_water_supply_
  strategy.aspx
Steelhead and Salmon Recovery
  http://www.dfw.state.or.us/fish/CRP/upper_willamette_river_plan.asp
Willamette Mission State Park Side Channel Reconnection
  http://www.willamette-riverkeeper.org/WRK/documents/mission-bottom-
  channel-restoration.pdf
Willamette River Basin Water Quality
  http://www.deq.state.or.us/about/eqc/agendas/attachments/2009oct/F-
  WillametteBasinAssessmentRpt.pdf
Willamette River Habitat Protection and Restoration Program
  www.nwcouncil.org/fw/projectselection/BiOp/200901200.pdf

Restoration/Conservation Initiatives and Groups

Cascade Pacific Resource Conservation & Development
    http://www.cascadepacific.org/water.htm
Freshwaters Illustrated
    http://www.freshwatersillustrated.org/
Freshwater Trust
    http://www.thefreshwatertrust.org/
Greenbelt Land Trust
    http://www.greenbeltlandtrust.org/
Meyer Memorial Trust: Willamette River Initiative
    http://www.mmt.org/willamette-river-basin-restoration
Oregon Watershed Enhancement Board
    http://www.oregon.gov/OWEB/index.shtml
    http://cms.oregon.gov/OWEB/Pages/SIP_Willamette.aspx
Pacific Northwest Ecosystem Research Consortium
    http://oregonstate.edu/dept/pnw-erc/
Society for Ecological Restoration
    http://www.ser.org/
Willamette Partnership
    http://willamettepartnership.org/
Willamette Riverkeeper
    http://www.willamette-riverkeeper.org/

Recreation

Portland Parks and Recreation (Map)
    http://www.portlandonline.com/parks/
Oregon Parks and Recreation Department Water Trails
    http://www.oregon.gov/oprd/BIKE/Pages/other_recreation.aspx
Recreation Guide
    http://www.portlandonline.com/ohwr/
Willamette River Water Trail
    http://www.willamettewatertrail.org/

Acknowledgements

I am full of gratitude for the people who offered their wisdom and support during this project. First, to my husband, Ben: Thank you for not falling when I leaned so heavily on you, when I read you ugly drafts. Thank you for your gentle honesty. Thank you for asking me to go kayaking on the Willamette some years ago, when we were younger and didn't have a mortgage payment or so many cares.

My parents deserve thanks for taking me to the Willamette as a child. These early experiences awakened a love for this river. Dad, thank you for teaching me how to identify my first bird, the white-crowned sparrow. Mom, thank you for teaching me that something as ordinary as picking blueberries can be an adventure. I am blessed to be surrounding by people so in love with the world's abundant beauty.

I thank Kathleen Dean Moore, for her enduring support and encouragement. Kathleen first listened to my idea for a research project and suggested I write a book about the Willamette. I followed her advice and undertook a project that inspired me to think about the world in new ways. I could not have written a single essay without her wisdom, insight, and sharp eye.

Dr. Lori Cramer and Dr. Stan Gregory both provided much-needed direction. Historian and scientist Patricia Benner spent considerable time with me. Her passion for the Willamette River and library of historical knowledge were essential to this project. Blessed are the wonderful, wise women of my writing group. They played a major role in the editing process, and their kind feedback made these essays better. Thank you for listening and, most importantly, for caring.

To the OSU Press—I am indebted to your expertise and dedication. Mary Braun met with me repeatedly during the review process, answering my questions even when they were far outside her job description. Thank you for believing in my potential, for your patience, for your sincerity. Micki Reaman helped transform this project from manuscript to book in my mind. Jo Alexander and her editing magic improved these pages tremendously. And while I didn't work with him directly, Tom Booth no doubt was orchestrating the entire process. I am so proud to have the OSU Press insignia on this book.